MW00987429

In the Language of

Walter Benjamin

Carol Jacobs

In the Language of
Walter Benjamin

The Johns Hopkins University Press

BALTIMORE AND LONDON

© 1999
The Johns Hopkins University Press
All rights reserved
Published 1999
Printed in
the United States of America
on acid-free paper
9 8 7 6 5 4 3 2 1

The Johns Hopkins University Press
2715 North Charles Street
Baltimore, Maryland 21218-4363
www.press.jhu.edu

Library of Congress
Cataloging-in-Publication Data
will be found
at the end of this book.
A catalog record for this book is available
from the British Library.

ISBN 0-8018-6031-8

For Henry:

Paris, Berlin, Buffalo, Baltimore,

Myslowitz, Braunschweig, Marseille

Contents

Acknowledgments

I would like to thank those whose warm and insistent invitations to write and speak on Benjamin over the years led me to believe that I might yet have something more to say: Ian Balfour, Cynthia Chase, David Ferris, Anselm Haverkamp, and Christiaan L. Hart Nibbrig. My thanks to Willis Regier, who greeted the possibility of this project with unprecedented generosity and enthusiasm and who saw it through with exceptional professionalism. I am enormously grateful to Carolyn Moser for her intelligent and meticulous work as a copyeditor. My special thanks to Jill Robbins, whose steadfast encouragement about this volume would have been surprising had I not already been spoiled by her remarkable brand of intellectual friendship over the years.

Parts of this book first appeared in *Modern Language Notes* (December 1971 and December 1975), *Diacritics* (Fall–Winter 1992), *Studies in Romanticism* (Winter 1992), and Christiaan Hart-Nibbrig, ed., *Übersetzen: Walter Benjamin* (Frankfurt: Suhrkamp, 1998). My thanks to the Trustees of Boston University for permission to reprint the materials from *Studies in Romanticism*.

Abbreviations

References to the collected works of Walter Benjamin in German (Walter Benjamin, *Gesammelte Schriften,* ed. Rolf Tiedemann and Hermann Schweppenhäuser [Frankfurt: Suhrkamp, 1972]) are marked with the volume number in Roman numerals, usually followed by a book number in arabic numerals, and finally with the page number in arabic numerals. Page numbers for any English translations consulted follow. The English translations are sometimes modified only slightly, and sometimes radically. The abbreviations used in citing the translations are as follows:

BC   *Berlin Chronicle,* in *Reflections,* ed. Peter Demetz (New York: Harcourt Brace Jovanovich, 1978), 3–60.

BCh   "Berlin Childhood ca 1900," unpublished translation by Shierry Weber Nicholson

DS   "Doctrine of the Similar," trans. Knut Tarnowski, *New German Critique,* no. 17 (Spring 1979): 65–69.

HiM   "Hashish in Marseille," in Demetz, *Reflections,* 137–45.

IP   "Image of Proust," in *Illuminations,* ed. Hannah Arendt, trans. Harry Zohn (New York: Schocken, 1969), 201–15.

MF   "On the Mimetic Faculty," in Demetz, *Reflections,* 333–36.

N   "N [Re the Theory of Knowledge, Theory of Progress]," in *Benjamin: Philosophy, Aesthetics, History,* ed. Gary Smith (Chicago: University of Chicago Press, 1983), 43–83.

OGTD   *The Origin of German Tragic Drama,* trans. John Osborne (London: NLB, 1977).

OLaS   "On Language as Such and on the Language of Man," in Demetz, *Reflections,* 314–32.

S   "Surrealism," in Demetz, *Reflections,* 177–92.

TH   "Theses on the Philosophy of History" (a title translated in my text as "On the Concept of History"), in Arendt, *Illuminations,* 253–64.

TT   "The Task of the Translator," in Arendt, *Illuminations,* 69–82.

In the Language of
Walter Benjamin

One

Letters from Walter Benjamin

No. Walter Benjamin never wrote to me. He took his own life, died before I was born. Perhaps this goes without saying, and yet it has little or nothing to do with historical chronology. For, more or less, this is so of any writer with respect to any reader. We must learn to regard what comes to us from Benjamin, then, as something other than expression (*Aussage*) or direct communication (*Mitteilung*) (iv.1.9; TT, 69). Isn't this what Benjamin's "The Task of the Translator" suggests by telling us that "no poem is intended for the reader, no image for the beholder, no symphony for the listener" (iv.1.9; TT, 69), by telling us that no piece of writing, neither translation nor original, communicates very much to the reader "who understands it" (iv.1.9; TT, 69)? For Benjamin it is always a question of, and questioning of, understanding. Less perhaps of *under*-standing, as the inevitable English translation would have it (for *understanding* proposes a relation between reader and text in which one might position oneself properly and solidly with respect to an object) than of *Ver*-stehen, a dispersal of that certainty of stance.

The essays that follow were written over the span of an academic life-time. They are the intermittent attempts from the late sixties through the early nineties in which I tried to understand Benjamin, or rather, to understand his work, to come to terms with it, though never as a totality. I would like to believe he taught me how to read in the practice of this interrupted intention and taught me that reading is, necessarily, the practice of interrupting intention. The process of contemplation that these essays perform, then, is marked by an unceasing pausing for breath (sometimes for many years). The impulse of the ever-renewed recommencement might offer a justification for the irregular rhythm of the book, its fragmentation into seemingly capricious parts. Yet, just so it is apparent what we are about here, fragmentation, for Benjamin, has little to do with chapter breaks: "It is characteristic of writing," he writes, "to start and stop with every new sentence" (1.1.209; OGTD, 29), and sometimes, in Benjamin, more often than that.

And yet I feel obligated in this, the introductory chapter, to offer, as we are systematically asked to do, the "fundamental conception" of the book. To be sure, Benjamin tells us, "the value of thought fragments is all the more decisive the *less* they are able to directly measure themselves according to the fundamental conception" (1.1.208; OGTD, 29). And here there is, certainly, no direct cohesion or measure. For however didactic in tone the writing sometimes becomes, these essays lack the validity of an instruction which could be asserted by virtue of its own authority.

Still, I would like to make a certain claim, if not to authority, then to truth, at least to truth as Benjamin understood it. He was careful to view truth (*Wahrheit*) as bound to its *Darstellung*—that is, its presentation, performance, production—an untranslatable term, really, which will appear here, therefore, often in the foreignness of Benjamin's native tongue. And he was just as careful to distinguish truth from knowing (*Erkennen*) or knowledge (*Erkenntnis*). The Darstellung of truth is not to be conceived of as mediating an acquisition that might be caught as in a spider's web, a truth that might come flying into it from outside. If, for knowledge, method is a way of possessing its object, if its very object is determined by the fact that it must be taken possession of—for *truth*, the method is Darstellung of itself.

There is, accordingly, no knowledge that one might catch hold of in the pages to come.[1] Benjamin insists that truth escapes projection into the realm of knowledge: it is grasped, rather, he tells us, at every turn, through the most precise immersion in the minute detail of subject matter. And this is the path I have followed: it is one of detour, digression, even ruse, but also one in which I have taken Benjamin's text, in all its details, at its word, literally. While the process of thinking may repeatedly begin anew here, it always returns in a roundabout way to its original task, that of being true to Benjamin's writing by following the performance (Darstellung) of his prose. And how does one account for the performance of another's writings if not by producing a performance of one's own? The reader, forced to pause and reflect, joins the read in the act, the enactment, the production of interpretation.

There are many names that Benjamin gives us for his *Darstellungen* and the performances he in turn demands of us. "Translation," "citation," "plagiarism" come immediately to mind. These are translations, then, but translations that, rather than making his writings comfortably our own, let the reading be violently moved by the foreignness of Benjamin. And yes, in a sense they are plagiarisms, and certainly citations. As Benjamin's narrator more or less declares in the opening lines of "Myslowitz—Braunschweig—Marseille," what you have read so far is, for the most part, not by me. That is to say that I have plagiarized shamelessly, often citing Benjamin without, by appropriate punctuation, marking the border between his text and mine.[2] Translation, citation, plagiaristic copy: these are just a few of the concepts that traditionally promise a reproduction and possession that Benjamin will graze tangentially in order to pursue his own course. I have performed them without shame because for Benjamin both citation and plagiarism have their place, not only in the short story just cited but also, for example, in *Trauerspiel,* where Benjamin's dream was to create a patchwork text of citations, or in "On the Concept of History," where citation functions as an act of reading that redeems the past.

In a sense, reading Benjamin is inevitably an attempt to redeem him—though, certainly, to rearticulate his work does not mean "to recognize 'it as it really was' " (1.2.695; TH, 255). Much in Benjamin speaks to the contrary. This is nowhere more evident than in piecing together, or rather side by side, the different kinds of text at issue in *Trauerspiel.* For if these opening pages rehearse the presentation of "philosophical writing"[3] as it appears in the "Epistemo-critical Prologue," later Benjamin speaks similarly of "allegorical Trauerspiel" and then again of "philosophical criticism" in relation to the work of art. Each of these has its redeeming qualities, and none saves its object in any predictable manner.

Thus, we are told, philosophical truth, elaborated by Plato as the content (*Gehalt*) of the beautiful, does not come forth in an act of unveiling. Nor does Benjamin, as he speaks of Plato, unveil (and thereby destroy) the secret of what Plato has to say, but performs, rather, in a simile the refusal of such disclosure. The content of the beautiful does not come to light "in an uncovering [*Enthüllung*] but rather shows itself in a process [*Vorgang*] which one might allegorically [*gleichnishaft*] designate as a bursting into flames of the covering [*Hülle*] on entering the realm of ideas, as a burning up of the work in which its form achieves its high point of illumination" (1.1.211; OGTD, 31). It is this,

Benjamin goes on to insist, that most dazzlingly demonstrates the difference between truth and a cognition out to possess its object.

More concretely, as he writes of the tasks of philosophy and of the "salvation of phenomena by means of ideas" (1.1.214; OGTD, 34), the empirical integrity of phenomena is never preserved.

> Phenomena, however, do not enter the realm of ideas whole, in their crude empirical state, adulterated by appearance [*Schein*], but rather redeemed [*gerettet*] only in their elements. Broken up into parts [*aufgeteilt*] they are deprived of their false unity in order to take part [*teilzuhaben*] in the genuine unity of truth. In this their disintegration [*Aufteilung*], phenomena are subordinated to concepts; the latter are what bring about the dissolution of things into their elements. (1.1.213–14; OGTD, 33)

Broken up, disintegrated, phenomena are neither incorporated nor contained in ideas. If the empirical wholeness of phenomena is given up, this is not to say that philosophy plots an escape beyond the empirical. Brought about in the same stroke that "saves" phenomena, the Darstellung of ideas, that other originary task of philosophy, takes place in the medium of and by means of the empirical. For ideas cannot and do not present themselves (*sich darstellen*) in themselves, "but rather solely and exclusively in an ordering of material [*dingliche*] elements in the concept. And they do this as the *configuration* of the elements" (1.1.214; OGTD, 34, emphasis added).

The ordering of elements in the Darstellung of ideas takes place as "configuration." Benjamin goes on, then, to offer us a figure, yet another gesture in which his refusal of naturally proper meaning in names is performed. In the configuration, the figure, the constellation, the idea operates as the "objective interpretation" of phenomena. The significance of the idea, he writes,

> may be illustrated with an analogy [*Vergleich*]. Ideas relate to things [*Dingen*] as constellations [*Sternbilder*] to stars. That means . . . [ideas] do not serve for knowledge of phenomena and in no way can [phenomena] be criteria for the existence of ideas. . . . The idea, the objective interpretation of phenomena— or rather of their elements—determines the relationship of the

phenomena to each other. Ideas are timeless constellations, and by virtue of the elements' being grasped as points in such constellations, phenomena are broken up and at the same time redeemed. (1.1.214–15; *OGTD*, 34)

The constellation, the spatial relationship among its points, is in no way a repository for the individual stars; the idea in no way a repository for empirical phenomena; just as Benjamin's figure disarticulates the connection between his language and its ostensible object. For Benjamin rejects here as elsewhere the romantic sense of "symbolic" language, with its promise of unity of appearance and being (*Erscheinung und Wesen*) (1.1.336; *OGTD*, 160). The opening pages of "Allegory and Trauerspiel" make this explicit. What Benjamin counters to this tyrannical and usurpatory (1.1.336; *OGTD*, 159) notion of the symbol is, of course, allegory. "No starker antithesis to the art symbol, the plastic symbol, the image of organic totality, is thinkable than this amorphous fragment as which the allegorical written image [*Schriftbild*] shows itself" (1.1.351–52; *OGTD*, 176). And no starker contrast to conventional concepts of critical prose than Benjamin's mode of writing. For Benjamin practices the practices of which he writes, from the very beginning. Thus, the opening line of *Trauerspiel*—"It is characteristic of philosophical writing with every turn, anew, to confront the question of *Darstellung*" (1.1.207; *OGTD*, 27, emphasis added)—opens a volume whose every turn inexorably confronts that question. As he takes for his object philosophical writing, the allegory of tragic drama, and, later, it goes without saying, philosophical criticism, there is no way to distinguish the ostensible object of his contemplation from the text that integrates it and thereby disintegrates.

In Benjamin's writing, then, which takes digression as its method, there is a rejection of outwardly directed communication and of knowledge, in the name of truth; a dearth of intention or, at the very least, a repeated renunciation of its uninterrupted flow. If he offers us an objective interpretation of certain phenomena, no knowledge is proffered therein. His "philosophical contemplation" makes unceasing pauses for breath, presenting its material in the capricious fragmentation of a mosaic that lacks any grounding conceptualization.

It is impossible to take proper account of all that goes on here—even and especially when Benjamin goes on to write of the history that

Trauerspiel stages and the philosophical criticism that takes that art form (or any art form) as its object. Just as phenomena are not incorporated whole in their objective interpretation in ideas, just as stars are not preserved in the configurations of the constellation, so nature in the productions of tragic drama can make no claim to eternal life.

> When history wanders onto the scene of Trauerspiel, it does so as writing [*Schrift*]. The word "history" stands on the countenance of nature in the sign-writing of transience. The allegorical physiognomy of the nature-history which is put on stage by means of the Trauerspiel, is really present as ruin. In the ruin, history has materially [*sinnlich*] distorted itself into the scene. And, figured in this manner [*so gestaltet*], history does not assume the form of the process of an eternal life so much as that of irresistible decay. . . . Allegories are in the realm of thoughts, what ruins are in the realm of things. (1.1.353–54; OGTD, 177)

Nature in Trauerspiel is that which has already become history—as written signs that mark the mortality of that which they ostensibly name. Therefore nature-history appears on the stage as ruin, as a process of ceaseless fall. No thing, then, stands redeemed as such in the history of Trauerspiel's writing, in its allegorical productions. Trauerspiel countenances only decay and transience, the realm of thought pervaded by ruin.[4]

And when Benjamin describes "philosophical criticism," what must evidently appear as his own enterprise, like philosophical contemplation in general and like allegorical Trauerspiel, criticism brings about a mortification of its object. The ruin and decay assigned to nature-history when staged by tragic drama, reappears here as critical writing. Transforming historical content into truth content, criticism "saves" the work of art only at the price of its "mortification" (1.1.357; OGTD, 182).

> It is the object of philosophical criticism to show that the function of the art form is precisely this: to make historical content [*Sachgehalt*] as it forms the basis of every significant work into philosophical truth content. This transformation [*Umbildung*] of content to truth content makes the decay [*Verfall*] of the effect, in which from decade to decade the attraction of earlier

charms decreases, into the ground of a rebirth in which all
ephemeral beauty falls away completely and the work holds its
own as ruin. In the allegorical construct of the baroque Trauerspiel, such fragmentary forms of the saved work of art have always marked themselves off clearly. (1.1.358; OGTD, 182)

Criticism, therefore, at once shows the work to be a ruin in which
factual content has fallen away and makes of the art form such a ruin. It
is as though criticism were already in the work of art as its potential.

What does it mean to read Benjamin, given his digressions on art,
philosophy, and criticism? This is the question I have been circling in
what, to be sure, is less an introduction, a leading directly into the
chapters to follow, than an elaborate detour by way of that difficult
work, *Trauerspiel*. Touching it at several points, like tangents a circle,
this fragmentary reading of fragments nevertheless might, it is hoped,
offer insights into the critical, philosophical, and even literary works of
Benjamin we approach here. (And given his definition of *truth*, who
would venture to distinguish among them?) Still, this is not because
things are identical in his writings: nothing returns in precisely the same
way, not even, say, when we read, once again, of constellations (in
"Doctrine of the Similar" [11.1.206; DS, 66]) or of criticism (in "The Task
of the Translator" [IV.1.15; TT, 76]). It is an error to search Benjamin's
work for stability in terminology. Nothing works devoid of context,
performance. These are texts that must always be read anew, less for the
referents they seem to preserve than for their Darstellung: here lives,
works, theories, terms, are saved only like phenomena in ideas, only like
stars in a constellation. Almost to the point, as Benjamin says of allegory, that all that is used to signify, "the signifying props" in his writing,
inevitably point "to something else" (1.1.351; OGTD, 175). "Any person,
any thing, any relationship can mean absolutely anything else" (1.1.350;
OGTD, 175). This is no more a matter for melancholy than it is for
linguistic exuberance. Best to think of it as the "intermittent rhythm of
a constant pause, the sporadic change of direction" (1.1.373; OGTD, 197)
he celebrates in allegory.

If I were true to Benjamin's sense of writing, rather than this attempt
at orientation, I should, perhaps, let my readers go astray in the chapters
to come. Benjamin understood and turned to the art of straying. And
yet, the next chapter begins and the last ends in more or less the same

place, the not-quite-Eden of a certain garden. Chapter 2 opens with a scene from Benjamin's autobiographical *Berlin Chronicle* in the curiously inscribed zoological gardens [*Tiergarten*] of his Berlin childhood; Chapter 6 closes with a meditation on the relation between the biblical Eden and certain postlapsarian practices of reading in relation to the Fall. This may well tell you less where we are than where we are not.

We are not in paradise: but in a sense we never stray entirely away from the origin—that is, *Ursprung*—as Benjamin spoke of it. It was, of course, above all, once again, in his habilitation thesis that Benjamin felt called upon to speak of origin—in that ill-fated dissertation that failed to grant him entry into the promised (if dreaded) land of the German academy, end-goal of the educational system he had so violently questioned in his youth. In a work entitled *Origin of German Tragic Drama* (*Ursprung des deutschen Trauerspiels*) the radical redefinition of "origin" cannot help but say something of where Benjamin himself stood. *Ursprung* (origin), he is quick to tell us, must not be confused with a coming into being, genesis, *Entstehung:* "Origin, though a thoroughly historical category, nevertheless has nothing in common with coming into being. In [the term] origin [*Ursprung*], no becoming of that which has come into being [*des Entsprungenen*] is intended, but rather that which arises out of becoming *and* passing away. Origin stands in the flow of becoming as a whirlpool and rips the material of genesis into its rhythmics" (1.1.226; OGTD, 45, emphasis added).

The "origin" is no path of progressive becoming. It has nothing in common with our common concept of origin. Within it, as the etymology of the term all too readily suggests, is an originary fissure, as *Ursprung*. Thus, it tears any sense of genesis or its materiality down into its eddy. *Ursprung* does not take place at the beginning; rather, the originary rupture of the *Ur-sprung* arises out of becoming *and* vanishing. It is neither the seeming progress of the one nor the decay of the other but must be thought of as springing forth in the side by side of both.

> The original [*das Ursprüngliche*] never gives itself to be recognized [*erkennen*] in the naked and manifest existence [*Bestand*] of the real [*Faktischen*] and its rhythmics stand open only to a *double insight*. [The original] wishes to be recognized on the one hand as restoration, as reestablishment, on the other as precisely what is therein imperfect and uncompleted. . . . The lines of di-

rection [*Richtlinien,* or less literally translated, "guiding princi-
ples"] of philosophical contemplation are traced out in the dialectic which inhabits the origin. Out of this dialectic, singularity
[*Einmaligkeit*] and repetition shows itself [*sic*] conditioned by
one another in everything essential. (1.1.226; OGTD, 45–46, emphasis added)

We should never forget, although in the rhythm of things we inevitably do, that what Benjamin himself sets out to write is *the origin of*. . . To
write the origin is not to give the story of an organic, historical development, made manifest to the reader, nor to unveil the cause, reveal how
its object has come into being. Nor is the origin bound to the factual or
real. It is the performance of a dialectic in which the reader is bound to
see double: both the gesture towards a restoration of what seems to have
come before and, precisely within that move towards reestablishment,
the uncompletability of that gesture. Singularity never arises in and of
itself but only appears as the failure of a repetition that can never be
brought about, at least not completely.

It is not that this could possibly *explain* what takes place in the pages
that follow. Let us just say that this double dialectic is at play in each of
the works I have ventured to read. Benjamin never ceased to write the
origin, to perform the double dialectic torn between becoming and
vanishing, restoration and incompletion, repetition and singularity, in
which, one could be tempted to say, the factual is consumed, if it were
not already torn to shreds.

This might put into perspective the very different kinds of texts that
are written on in the chapters to come. On the one hand, there are texts
that seek to restore the past: autobiography (*Berlin Chronicle*), biography ("Towards the Image of Proust"), followed by the evident prob-
lematization of such attempts in the fictional autobiographical anecdote, of "Myslowitz—Braunschweig—Marseille." On the other hand,
there are three essays of Benjamin that theorize language. It would be all
too easy to see the first as the recovering of lives lost, the second as the
knowing renunciation of such gestures as Benjamin comes to terms
with what language really is. But the dialectic is always double. Thus, the
rhythmics of double insight pervade alike the essays on language and
the writings that claim a life.

Nothing claims a life more directly than that which poses as autobiography. Benjamin wrote a number of them, including *Berlin Chronicle,* the object of the next chapter. Yet no matter how many phenomena of the past are clearly saved therein, no text could more persistently disclaim that autobiography is what it is about. *Berlin Chronicle,* Benjamin tells us, is not autobiography, even when it articulates, as he puts it, the space of life. He rejects the sense of continuous temporal flow consistent with the usual narration of life for a spatial discontinuity in which what is preserved might at best be called moments or memory. And memory is no recuperation of past time. Not unlike the disintegration of phenomena in ideas, memory is the figuration that time assumes in the moment of remembering (vi.488; *BC,* 28). Life, he quite bluntly lets us know, is simply not the stuff of which this figuration is made (vi.488; *BC,* 28). Despite the specificity of the past to which Benjamin returns us—childhood forays in the park, calls on Aunt Lehmann, a Proustian experience of recall in the Café des Deux Magots, a visit to an antiquarian jeweler—*Berlin Chronicle* is less a repository for what has happened than its Darstellung.

And this performance is both accompanied by and interspersed with meditations on memory and its inextricable relation to language, writing, space. Nothing takes place here as it might on reading a map whose graphic image orients us concretely to the physical realm we inhabit. Side by side with such forms of substantial, biographical promise, those spectacles of replication (of which there are many), a labyrinth is bound to emerge. The chamber at its center is of no concern. Commemorative statues of royalty surge up before the young boy's eye, but also a magic maze of water script at their feet. Soon thereafter, there are other labyrinths, this time those on the blotter pages in school notebooks, the overlayered traces that leave behind his intentional writing for its excess. And another labyrinth, a "graphic schema of [Benjamin's] life" (vi.491; *BC,* 30) that marks no static picture but the ever-moving interweavings of his relationships with others, a page he seems to have produced but inevitably lost and was never able to reproduce. This much is certain about that leaf; it was not really Benjamin who wrote it, nor were its images really of people. Over and over in *Berlin Chronicle* people play but a ghostly role, and especially its apparent author, whose impotence is made explicit. Mortification of the textual object.

And how could it be otherwise? For Benjamin, remembrance is no instrument for digging up and taking hold of an external past. Memories are, rather, a medium in which debris and buried ruins are reinterred as one probes, a digging in which no thing is brought to the surface. And yet Benjamin hardly bemoans a loss of treasure, but celebrates, rather, the dark good fortune of the digging itself and even the failure to find.

Memory, he rarely lets us forget for long, takes place in language, just as Benjamin's prose is always a preserve of linguistic treasures to account for, as when the memories of his Aunt Lehmann and her glasslike voice generate a meditation on the fragile and potentially shattering relation between name and place. Language is no tool to catch hold of its referent. Just as going astray in a city requires rambling as in a wood (VI.469; BC, 8–9), the *Berlin Chronicle* calls on its readers who wander through it to listen for the strange cries of birds, the breaking of twigs underfoot, even its sudden silences. It is these that figure the text of self-contemplation in which Benjamin engages. It is this to which he puts his uncertain signature.

If at the center of *Berlin Chronicle* Benjamin openly renounces autobiography, no such declaration dispels the sense of conventionally biographical anecdote in "Towards the Image of Proust." The essay, whose title and text float between the "image" and the man, nevertheless offers us, however opaquely, some guidance as to what it is about. For Benjamin defines the image as an ever-increasing discrepancy between life and poetry, and it is this lesson that he repeats, differently, throughout. And yet the repetition of a lesson is not quite what takes place. What Benjamin does do over and over, in passages that seem to root us in life, is to perform the discrepancy between life and text, memory and forgetting, identity and similarity. As in *Berlin Chronicle*, a figuration or ornamentation arises in the moment of a remembering that is indistinguishable from forgetting.

But always, and again, out of the gesture towards restoration, the incompleteness therein inevitably emerges. Thus, in a well-known passage Benjamin will compare Proust's reach for the past, his "involuntary memory," to a children's game. The children transform a rolled-up stocking from the laundry chest, what seems a pouch with contents, into an empty stocking. Not that they yearn for its contents. What they desire and what they can never have enough of is the game of emptying.

And so for Proust, Benjamin tells us, whose language empties the self to bring in the image. And so for Benjamin, who plays a similar game with Proust's life.

Thus, Benjamin can speak yet again of Proust's *mémoire involuntaire* first as a shock of rejuvenation that reappropriates the past and, soon thereafter, as a monstrous act of aging that instantaneously consumes it. Our physiognomnic wrinkles, the portraits of our aging, are the recordings of an absence. The self is never at home to its own immediate experience. For Proust, Benjamin tells us, the quintessence of experience is to experience or learn how elusive knowledge and experience are. It is a learning, then, that is never experienced as knowledge; for remembering (also for the reader of this essay), inevitably gives way to forgetting, just as rejuvenation to aging or life to death.

And remembering inevitably gives way to language. For here, as elsewhere, Benjamin repeatedly brings us back to language. This is the fire in which the covering—of what seems life—bursts into flames and consumes itself. And yet, that is still imprecise. But the close of "Towards the Image of Proust" does remind us that the image arising from the discrepancy between life and loss, remembering and forgetting, rejuvenation and precipitous aging, emerges only in the "articulation of Proust's sentences" (II.1.314; IP, 205), an articulation that seemed towards the end to speak of death. If so, it is less that their syntax imitated the choking rhythm of an impending, asthmatic death than that Proust's sentences created that death. The double dialectic is not caught in an economy of asceticism, in a renunciation that sacrifices life in the name of the work. Rather, re-nunciation, or its staging, creates the illusion of something lost (*perdu*). As in the "Epistemo-Critical Prologue" if Benjamin submerges us in the rhythmics of the origin, we are also apprised of its theatricality.

That theatricality becomes all the more unmistakable in "Myslo-witz—Braunschweig—Marseille." For here is a piece framed in the playful vagaries of storytelling. From the very beginning, the possibility of putting one's signature to a text is something of a joke in a story where the narrators can prove their identities only by assuming or remembering the name of another. If *Berlin Chronicle* poses, however briefly or intermittently, as autobiography, as the recapitulation of the author's life, if "Towards the Image of Proust" seems to narrate biographical anecdotes of a novelist (who, granted, wrote fictional autobiography), the wit of "Myslowitz—Braunschweig—Marseille" is such that its auto-biographical tale makes little pretense to prelinguistic depths. And above all—or rather, all through—is a laughter questioning all that exists while staging an uncanny balancing act between consumption and renunciation. The narrator of the framed story appears on the scene much like the hemlock that silences the Socratic voice of reason, more or less indistinguishable from the hashish he ingests. And yet "Myslowitz—Braunschweig—Marseille" intoxicates, less as a unidirectional correction to either autobiography or fiction than as a constant alternation between dreamlike and waking states. The rhythm of the prose is such that we slip from name to name: names of authors, storytellers, artists, cities. Each promises a treasure of royal proportions. But the tale is predicated on the understanding that fortunes are always missed by a hair, especially those based on a concept of value like that of an authoritative name.

It is such a linguistic concept that Benjamin also marginalizes in his essay on translation. That marginalization takes place in "Myslowitz—Braunschweig—Marseille" as the narration collapses the distance between perceiver and perceived, namer and named. In *Berlin Chronicle,* "The Image of Proust," and "Myslowitz—Braunschweig—Marseille" the subject seems of issue: in "The Task of the Translator" ("Die Aufgabe des Übersetzers"), such is not the case. The translator is given up and abandoned as a matter of course, a surrender already evident in the German *Aufgabe,* though lost in the English translation.

And yet, the essay is not really about losing in translation—neither about loss of the subject nor loss of a significance the original might have claimed. Translation does not restitute meaning (no matter how often Benjamin inevitably lets us forget it). And how could it be otherwise when Benjamin insists that no work of literature is intended or fruitful for the understanding of the reader to begin with. Just as the idea does not serve for knowledge of phenomena, but rather, configures the relation of phenomena to each other, so translation does not preserve either the meaning or even the syntactical relations in the original, which, in turn, did not . . .

Still, with every turn we must reconfront the question of meaning, which never ceases, it seems, to flourish anew in our modes of writing and reading. In "Towards the Image of Proust" Benjamin performs that questioning by a shift, in passages that open with a term of promise and close with a term of refusal—a slip, say, from remembering to forgetting, from lived life to woven text, or from rejuvenation to instantaneous aging.

The Darstellung in "The Task of the Translator" is similar but not identical. For whereas the Proust essay will contrast two terms that normally maintain their individual, opposing meanings, here Benjamin translates. He translates (which is to say, disintegrates) the meanings we traditionally ascribe to each of its most significant terms, just when they promise to blossom forth the definition of translation. Still, restoration takes place ever anew as the eye of the reader necessarily reinstates meaning to a familiar vocabulary highly akin to conventional concepts of translation. In this way, we experience, repeatedly, how fleetingly sense attaches to such words as *original, life, nature, kernel, fruition, kinship, fidelity,* and *literality.* In these terms and others Benjamin lets "meaning [plunge] from abyss to abyss" (IV.1.21; TT, 82). Each word, its original sense shaken, becomes the uncertain ground for its own fragmentation into mosaic or ruin. Translation does not simply take us—or fail to take us—from one national language to another. This should at last make clear why letters from Walter Benjamin are not necessarily correspondence.

Although, to be sure, "Doctrine of the Similar" seems founded on the concept of correspondence. Whereas in "The Task of the Translator" words fail to correspond to their meanings (much less to parallel intentions in another, foreign tongue), in "Doctrine of the Similar" similarity is pitched to macrocosmic dimensions of space and time.

Just as *translation* is haunted by the meaning of an "original" and originary meaning, so *similarity* too is staged in a linear temporality. Benjamin offers a double history: that of the individual and that of human civilization, in each of which, he tells us, similarity had a critical role to play. In these genetic stories, however, rather than showing us similarities produced by history, Benjamin reproduces "the processes that engender such similarities" (II.1.204; DS, 65). As he does, though he casts his opening pages in a long series of befores and afters (childhood and adulthood, question and answer, "ancient peoples" and "modern human being[s]," the "course of time," "the course of . . . centuries," "historical development," objects followed by their imitations, stars by their interpretation, text by reader), his language engenders a mode of similarity that consumes such structures in a flash. Implicit in this is a

shock to our concepts of history and interpretation, a shock all the
more unmistakable in the last piece Benjamin was to write, "On the
Concept of History." Explicit is a crystallization of language as "non-
sensuous similarity" in which the relation of thing, name, and letter will
never be the same again.

And yet, thing and name, it would seem, were once the same, at least
"in the beginning." With "On Language as Such" we are back at the
beginning, for we return, coincidentally, to one of Benjamin's earliest
pieces and to the Garden of Eden. We return as well to that original
story, story of the origin and of the origins of language, and to a figure
and time in which restoration and incompleteness therein could not
have been of consequence—at least insofar as we return to God. God's
language, with its absolute relation to cognition, at once creates and
names. Adamic naming, however, is not creative but rather a naming
according to knowledge, and so is not quite the same—even when in the
act of naming Eve, Adam participates most perfectly in divine infinity.
How do we speak of the link between God's language and human
language, which in a sense precipitates the way in which autobiography,
biography, and translation, for example, speak to us? Benjamin has
a word to mark the difference between God's creative language and
Adamic naming: *conception* (*Empfängnis*). "Conception" is at once that
which links God to the human and what differentiates the human
capacity to name from God's creative word. As Adam speaks, conception marks the point of articulation between name and thing.

Lost in the multiple echoes of "conception," our reading, here more
than in any previous passage in the book, goes off on a tangent. Still
(since the laws of remembrance are at play even in the critical text), it is
a tangent that touches the most crucial issues of the book: self-naming,
language, interpretation, and redemption. A strange and unwieldy constellation emerges from reading "On Language as Such": conception,
translation, immaculate conception, Eve, the Virgin Mary, typological
reading, redemption, and woman. An unlikely constellation. But then
again, Benjamin writes, "any relationship can mean absolutely anything
else" (1.1.350; *OGTD*, 175). And this puts much that has taken place into
perspective, even if, from this vantage point, we see all too clearly why
letters from Benjamin tend to arrive without his proper signature, if
they can be said to arrive at all.

Two

Berlin Chronicle
Topographically Speaking

Letter to Walter Benjamin

Dear Walter:

Your last letter, in which to my joy I found at least some biographical information about you, lies before me, and I implore you to realize that in this regard you can never do too much of a good thing for me. . . .

Accept my most cordial regards and pardon my brevity on such a boundless subject. If you cannot or will not reply, send me at least a picture postcard with your photo and autograph.

In the winter of 1932, or perhaps earlier, Benjamin began a series of passages he entitled *Berlin Chronicle*. By the fall of that year, his editors tell us, Benjamin may or may not have finished the *Chronicle* and have turned to transforming pieces of it into *Berlin Childhood around 1900* (VI.799). In a letter of February 28, 1933, Benjamin wrote to Gershom Scholem that *Berlin Childhood* might be considered finished, since he had just composed the last piece—"serially the first."[1] Yet that passage, entitled "Tiergarten," had appeared almost a month earlier in the *Frankfurter Zeitung*. Moreover, another version of it was serially also the first of the *Berlin Chronicle*, so that if we are to believe the history of that earlier text, "Tiergarten" was already at least partially composed in 1932.

If the speculations on dating the *Chronicle* lead us into something of a maze, this is no less the case with the order of its pages. Scholem, the first editor of the manuscript, puzzles over the way in which Benjamin "for no explicable reasons jumps . . . repeatedly over a page"[2] and also upsets the "natural order of the pages" on a number of occasions, so that content and transition force one to move back and forth in reading. Scholem goes on to surmise that a page, at least, must have been lost. This would explain the fact that whereas Benjamin speaks of five guides who introduced him to the city, Scholem can find only three, the second and the third seemingly having gone astray with the lost leaf. The editors of the *Collected Works,* Rolf Tiedemann and Hermann Schweppenhäuser, however, insist on finding the missing guides "very well named" (VI.804) within the pages at hand for anyone who knows how to read.

The impossibility of chronological certainty in the biographical facts, the problematic continuity of the passages, the question of the lost page—all these may seem extraneous issues (though not quite as outrageously extraneous as another to which we will come, the name of the woman who, years later, was the first to decipher the manuscript of the *Berlin Chronicle:* Steinschneider).[3] And yet each of these issues enters *Berlin Chronicle* at crucial moments. We might call them primal "entrances into the labyrinth" (VI.491; BC, 31), the "reading labyrinth" (IV.1.278) that is at once Benjamin's life and text. For it is the author himself who explicitly distinguished the *Berlin Chronicle* from autobiography:

> Memories even when they go on extensively do not always present [*darstellen*] an autobiography. And here it is certainly not one, not even of the Berlin years, the only ones in question [*Rede*]. For autobiography has to do with time, with lapse [*Ablauf*] and with what makes up the continuous flow of life. Here it is a matter of space, moments, the discontinuous. For even if months and years emerge here, it is in the figure they have in the moment of remembering. (VI.488; BC, 28)

Is this not Benjamin's answer before the question to those who seek an uninterrupted flow of text and a factual, ordered representation of life? The *Berlin Chronicle* is not a chronicle, if that term suggests the "continuous register of events in order of time; a historical record . . . in which the facts are narrated without philosophic treatment, or any attempt at literary style" (OED). What poses as an autobiographical work is one of the many detours the contemplation begun in *The Origin of German Tragic Drama* has taken. It is no coincidence, therefore, that in *Berlin Chronicle* too, as in the habilitation thesis, it is a question of Darstellung: ("Memories . . . do not always present [*darstellen*] an autobiography.")

Darstellung ("representation," "presentation," "performance"), Benjamin tells us, is *the* characteristic question that philosophy must continually confront.[4] "It is characteristic of philosophical writing, at every turn, to confront the question of *Darstellung* anew" (1.1.207; OGTD, 27). In the philosophical treatise, "renunciation of the uninterrupted flow of intention is its primary characteristic. Persistently, thinking always begins anew; in a roundabout way it goes back to the matter [*Sache*] itself. This unremitting drawing of breath is the most inherent form-of-existence of contemplation" (1.1.208; OGTD, 28).

Darstellung takes place in an intermittent, broken rhythm, as an unceasing brokenness of breath. This is the method of the treatise or esoteric essay that Benjamin offers as exemplary of his own treatise entitled *The Origin of German Tragic Drama* and apparently of *Berlin Chronicle* as well, where Benjamin also renounces "continuous flow" for the rhythm of interruption. Of the treatise Benjamin writes, "Darstellung is the epitome of its method. Method is digression [*Umweg*]. Darstellung as digression" (1.1.208; OGTD, 28). Benjamin's method is also Darstellung as *Umweg*, representation or performance as digression, detour, ruse—digression, detour, and ruse in which it is a question of space, moments, discontinuities (VI.488; BC, 28). *Berlin Chronicle* is performed as a collection of disconnected snapshots (*Augenblicksaufnahmen*).[5] Like those disparate picture postcards Benjamin was wont to send Siegfried Kracauer, among others, through the early 1930s, they are sent to us from another time, another place, or rather other times and other places. One ponders whether to view the images or read the writing and wonders wherein the difference might lie.[6]

This relation between image and writing is the central point of the first fragment of that larger fragment entitled *Berlin Chronicle*. "Serially the first," biographically the last, the opening passage is a primal entrance and yet already a detour and ruse that nevertheless leads us into the "story labyrinth" (VI.515; BC, 56):

> But at the end of Bendler Street loomed the labyrinth which was not lacking its Ariadne: the maze surrounding Friedrich Wilhelm III and Queen Luise who on their image-covered pedes-

tals struggled right out of the flower beds as though turned to stone by the magic strokes that a small canal wrote in the sand. Rather than to the figures, my eyes turned to the pedestal because what was happening there—even if unclearer in its context [*Zusammenhang*]—was nearer in space. (vi.465; *bc*, 3).

Hardly have we entered the maze than we arrive at what *Berlin Childhood* calls "the goal" (iv.1.237): Friedrich Wilhelm and Queen Luise.[7] And yet, in this originary, though not Edenic, garden, at the center of the labyrinth, lies another labyrinth, the writing in the sand of a small stream of water, whose magic strokes have had a startling effect. This writing, it would seem, has the Medusa-like power to transform the human into realistic figures of stone.[8] For this reason, perhaps, the child looks neither at those magic signs nor at the lifelike representations of the rulers (iv.1.237) but deflects his eyes instead to the images at the base of those figures. Benjamin remains silent on the object of his glance, yet at least one guide to the city of Berlin describes these as child-filled scenes "symbolizing . . . the enjoyments of the Thiergarten."[9] There is no escape for this child in the Tiergarten, after all, from the powers of the Gorgon, but also no coherent representation of the particular onlooker. Clarity and coherence are sacrificed in the name of a certain space, Benjamin tells us, which—in anticipation—we might call a memorial stone.

Caught in the folds of the Tiergarten labyrinth, then, we find at its center not only the historical, celebratory figures of Friedrich Wilhelm and Luise—the statuary version of biography—but also the seemingly accidental writing that has the power both to petrify the rulers and to deflect the eye of the observer to another mode of image cut in stone. That the gaze is inevitably detoured among these in their intertwined relations prefigures the entanglements of what is to come.

This much should be clear. Benjamin's place for viewing is middle of the labyrinth.

Probably one will never become master of anything in which one has not known impotence, and whoever concurs in that will also know that this impotence does not lie at the outset or before all endeavor with respect to the matter, but rather at its center. I am coming then to the center of my Berlin life . . . : impotence with

respect to the city. It was doubly grounded: first in a very poor
sense of orientation; if it took thirty years until knowledge of left
and right became flesh and blood, until I made out how the map
of a city is used, knowledge [*Wissen*] about this ineptitude was
still far from familiar.(vi.466; *BC*, 4).

How shall we understand this unconsciousness, this inability to orient
his body or decipher a map, and especially the phrasing that equates a
visceral sense of direction in one's body with the ability to read a map of
Berlin? And all this doubled and compounded by a subsequent failure
to recognize his first failure of knowledge? Caught in the middle of both
Berlin and life (one begins to suspect they are almost interchangeable),
Benjamin doesn't know which way to turn. If he indeed learns to read
the city map, he does not necessarily master reading himself; knowledge
about his ineptitude remains unfamiliar.

But perhaps finding his way is not Benjamin's goal after all, nor
merely its contrary.

Not to find one's way in a city—that could be uninteresting and
banal. Unawareness is needed, beyond that, nothing. But to go
astray in a city—as one goes astray in a wood—that already requires a completely different schooling. Then signboards, street
names, passersby, roofs, kiosks, or taverns must speak to the individual forced to wander like a breaking twig under foot in the
wood, like the terrified cry of a bittern from afar, like the sudden
silence of a clearing in the middle of which a lily shoots up. Paris
taught me this art of straying: it fulfilled the dream whose earliest traces were the labyrinths on the blotter leaves of my school
notebooks. (vi.469; *BC*, 8–9).

Should the city speak as Benjamin would have it, speak (transformed by
simile into its other) in the privileged mode reserved for those who have
gone astray as in a wood, then signs, names, people, and objects alike
cannot be read as one learns at school. They must, rather, be disarticu-
lated and disread, heard as a breaking, a shriek, an abrupt silence: no act
of translation can render these humanly articulate. Yet it is this, rather
than finding his way, that fulfills Benjamin's dream. There were earlier
signs of it, as always, for labyrinths, despite misleading indications

to the contrary, have no beginnings and no endings here. Benjamin's labyrinth points us towards the involutions on the blotting pages of his childhood copybooks: thus, another foliage replaces the simile of the wood (among so many metaphorical forests figured in the *Berlin Chronicle*); page and leaf (as in the half-forgotten English of another era) are inextricable in the German *Blatt*. Perhaps these "school notebooks" provide the "completely different schooling" that, we are told, makes possible going astray in a city as in a wood. The first traces of Benjamin's dream appear in the incidental script, the maze of fluid ink left not by what he purposefully penned in class, not by what remained on the written page, but by its excesses—magic lines layered one over another and side by side on leaves designed to blot rather than to preserve and delineate.[10] And this labyrinth is hardly distinguishable or at least inextricable[11] from those of the Tiergarten with its mazes of foliage and waterscript.

And yet "for many years," Benjamin writes, "actually, I have indeed been playing with the notion of articulating the space [*Raum*] of life—Bios—graphically in a map" (VI.466; *BC, 5*). Despite his disavowal of autobiography, despite his doubly grounded disorientation, intermittently and in flashes, Bios as graphic writing appears on the scene as an ironic possibility.[12]

> I think of an afternoon in Paris to which I owe insights into my life that overcame me in a flash with the power of an illumination. It was precisely this afternoon that my biographical relationships to people, my friendships [*Freundschaften*] and comradeships [*Kameradschaften*], my passions [*Leidenschaften*], and love affairs [*Liebschaften*] revealed themselves in their liveliest, most hidden [*verborgensten*], interweavings [*Verflechtungen*].
> (VI.490; *BC, 30*)

Are we then out of the woods, no longer lost in the labyrinth, grounded in "friendships"[13] at last in the biographical, which proves so elusive in *Berlin Chronicle*? As in the forest of that earlier passage, there is a strange language that speaks to us here, one that is silent or all but silenced for those who listen only for the integrity (rather than the breaking) of words and meaning. Its significance is confirmed by certain echoes one page later. The revelation that is crucial here leaves behind the static nouns of friendship, comradeship and so on (all marked in German by the suffix -*schaft*) to insist on the movement of their hidden interweavings (*Verflechtungen,* a gerund marked by the suffix -*ung*). It is less the passions and love affairs that interest Benjamin than their interconnectings, and it is these that will be marked down in the written life.

> I say to myself: it had to be in Paris where the walls and the quais, the asphalt, the collections and the debris, the railings and the squares, the arcades and the kiosks teach us such a strange language that our relationships to people in the loneliness that surrounds us, our sunkenness in that world of things, reach the depths of a sleep in which the dream-image awaits them, that reveals to them their true face. (VI.490; BC, 30)

The lightning-like revelation celebrates intertwinings rather than what is intertwined. This, then, is the face of our relationships, so sunken in a world of things as to become grammatically indistinguishable from them, revealed only in the dream-image of a deep sleep. But what fashions this image; who dreams it?

> I want to speak of this afternoon because it made so apparent [*kenntlich*] what kind of command it is that cities have over the fantasy and why the city, in which people most relentlessly make claims on one another . . . [allowing] no contemplative moment to the individual, takes its revenge in memories [*Erinnerungen*] and the veil that it has clandestinely [*im Verborgensten*] woven out of our lives shows less the images of the people than the arenas [*Schauplätze*] in which we met others or ourselves. (VI.490–91; BC, 30)

What has taken place in this auto-bio-graphy? It is not Benjamin who remembers the city and maps it out along with his life. At best, as we shall see, he leaves a space for a strange forest of trees to grow, a forest in which he, of necessity, must lose himself. Benjamin is here all but woven out of the city's remembrances—woven out while woven in. The city takes our lives and takes its revenge in a veil of memories produced from them in secret (*im Verborgenen*), for we now see clearly that the city, not the author, is the artisan of the "most hidden [*verborgensten*] inter-weavings" of which we read above (vi.490; *BC*, 30). Moreover, the images of people give way to the arenas of their encounters with others and themselves. People are displaced: they become outskirts to the city's privileging of "*Schauplätze*."[14] The images of *Schauplätze*, literally translated those "places to view," are the endless theaters that, one could claim, are the critical scene of *Berlin Chronicle* (and not just because the term turns up so often).

In the images of *Schauplätze* "the space of life [is articulated]—Bios-graphically" (vi.466; *BC*, 5). It is here that the hidden interweavings are revealed. To be sure, the main actors on these stages are not people: "The more often I come back to these memories, the less it appears incidental to me how slight a role people play in them" (vi.490; *BC*, 30). Thus, it can be no coincidence that at the moment of sudden illumination Benjamin forgets the person for whom he waits, as though the city's remembering and his forgetting of self and others were inextricably intertwined: "On that afternoon, then, of which I will speak, I was sitting in the interior space of the Café des Deux Magots . . . where I was waiting, I forget for whom" (vi, 491; *BC*, 30). "I forget for whom" is precisely who comes, and comes to an "I" who is equally marginalized, forgetful of self. For not only does the idea of mapping a life graphically come over Benjamin as from elsewhere; what he writes is also written by another hand: "There, all at once and with compelling force, the thought came over me to draw a graphic schema of my life, and I also already knew in the same moment exactly how that was to be done. It was a very simple question with which I searched through my past, and the answers drew themselves as if of their own accord on a page [*Blatt*] that I pulled out" (vi.491; *BC*, 30–31).

Perhaps it goes without saying that the page is lost, blotted out—in a sense the page whose absence Scholem couldn't help sensing—the page of autobiography in which the self as author was from the beginning out of the question: "One or two years later when I lost the page, I was inconsolable. Never again have I been able to produce it as it was formed [*entstand*] before me then, resembling a row of genealogical trees" (vi.491; *BC*, 31).[15] Benjamin is inconsolable, not over the loss of his past, but over the loss of the page: from that lost leaf (*Blatt*)—a wood of sorts in which to go astray—another blotter page (*Löschblatt*) labyrinth of unintentional writing: veil, city, autobiography in which the enigmatic center one might call self or fate is of no concern.

> Now, however, when I would wish once again to establish [*wiederherstellen*] its outline in thought, without precisely reproducing it [*wiederzugeben*], I would rather speak of a labyrinth. What is housed in the chamber of its enigmatic center, self or fate, should not concern me here, all the more so, however, the many entrances that lead to the interior. These entrances I call primal acquaintances; each one of them is a graphic symbol of my acquaintance with a person, whom I did not meet through other people but rather through relations of neighborhood [*Nachbarschaftverhältnisse*], familial relationship [*Verwandtschaft*], school comradeship [*Schulkameradschaft*], mix-up [*Verwechselung*], travel companionship [*Reisegenossenschaft*]. (vi.491; BC, 31).

The graphic symbols of primal acquaintance, the entrances to the labyrinth, are primal acquaintance as accident—moreover, they appear as a series of contexts for relationship upset once again by the seemingly accidental gerund among the static nouns—in this case, *Verwechselung*, "confusion," "mix-up," which leaves individual identity irrelevant.

If the individual identity is relegated to the shadows, language, here the graphic symbol (isn't this what Benjamin is telling us?), is always primal: even if (or perhaps inevitably) unintentionally found and accidentally lost, even if fundamentally impossible to reproduce, its origination never to be repeated and certainly not by the person who writes it down. Another hand weaves the text, puts forth the symbol, whose only face is a dream image revealed in the depths of sleep. Memory is woven by a concealed artisan in which the image of people is always, possibly, a question of mistaken identity and nevertheless our passageway to the past.

If the living individual—if life—is not the stuff of which memories or consciousness [*Eingedenken*] is made, how are we to understand the figures that haunt Benjamin's *Chronicle*?

> For even if months and years rise up here, it is in the figure [*Gestalt*] that they have in the moment of remembering [*Eingedenkens*]. This peculiar figure—one could call it fleeting or eternal—

in no case is the stuff of which it is made that of life. And that is divulged still less in the role that my own life will play here than in that of the people who in Berlin—whenever and whoever—were closest to me. (VI.488; BC, 28)

What, then, of those closest to Benjamin? How do they figure here? Who are they and how can we situate them in all this when we have clearly read that their role is slight, displaced by images loomed by the memories of another: "The atmosphere of the city that is here conjured grants them only a brief shadowy existence. They steal along its walls like beggars, rise up ghostlike in its windows to then disappear, sniff around thresholds like a genius loci, and when they even fill [*erfüllen*] whole quarters with their names, it is in the manner in which the name of the dead [fills] the memorial stone on his grave" (VI.488–89; BC, 28).

Like beggars, like ghosts, like a genius loci—Benjamin's similes progressively intensify the marginality and the depersonalization. With rapid gestures of discontinuity, in blinks of the eye, before we know it, he shifts from the space of life (they steal along its walls like beggars) to the other side, from an apparently human realm where possession and desire still reign to what appears in the name of place (*loci*), and even in the name of death's textual display of absence, the memorial stone.

To be sure, all this follows upon Benjamin's withdrawal from autobiography: "Here, however [we speak of] space, moments [*Augenblicke*], and the discontinuous" (VI.488; BC, 28), he had written, you remember. No doubt this makes the context clearer. Let me digress to apologize for not always tracing the *Chronicle* in order, for doubling back and skipping around, thus sometimes losing sight of such logical connections. It is difficult to orient ourselves in this text, even if we heed Benjamin's admonition to renounce the center, difficult to find points of entry, to locate a place for commentary as a vantage point from which to contemplate, a window, perhaps, a threshold that might open before us the slate of Benjamin's text. But these, after all, are the neither here nor theres, the borderlines from which all critical writing inevitably takes its place.

Even in the name of death, then. These figures of the *Berlin Chronicle* might fill entire neighborhoods with their name (as in the case of Aunt Lehmann in an earlier passage to which we have yet to come), but such moments of apparently sovereign influence occur in the manner in which the name of the dead fills the memorial stone, marking the areas as their burial site.[16] And thus it is with those closest to the author—and who was closer to Benjamin than his former, childhood self? Their place is delineated as such non-places between: windows, thresholds, gravestones.

And yet, as the saying goes, nothing is written in stone, and certainly not the tomb inscription that might fix the relation of the city to those who once inhabited it. It is impossible to determine whether the names of the dead bear witness to the city or the other way around, whether Benjamin, say, bears witness to Berlin or the city weaves the veil of memories. "Berlin . . . has, however, no less but rather more than many other [cities], the places and moments where it bears witness to the dead, shows itself filled [*erfüllt*] with the dead" (vi.489; *bc*, 28), filled with their names like the tombstone that at once memorializes and pronounces absent what is in the earth beneath. This, too, makes up Benjamin's labyrinth, not just the meanderings of city streets, not just the interweavings of personal relations that dead-end, or perhaps come alive, in the possibility of mistaken identity. And isn't this where we began?—with the ever-changing positions of witness and witnessed, of inscription and inscribed, in the labyrinth of the Tiergarten?

We began with these but no less the involutions of recollection and forgetting, for there is no path of memory here that is not crossed with forgetting. Nothing remembered if not half-forgotten, nothing present to mind if not also a dream, if not interrupted by what "Towards the Image of Proust" calls the "Penelope-work of forgetting." For Benjamin, the interweaving of remembering and forgetting that creates his passages leads seamlessly back and forth to its other version, in the interpenetration of life and death. Benjamin writes of childhood, and like Rilke before him, he writes of its indifferent openness to life and death:[17] "the memories of childhood . . . so difficult to grasp . . . so . . . like half-forgotten dreams. For childhood, which knows no preconceived opinion, also knows none for life. It comes to the realm of the dead where it projects into that of the living, just as preciously connected . . . as to life itself" (vi.489; *bc*, 28).

It is these thresholds, then, that Benjamin haunts: the locus of the interweavings (*Veflechtungen*) (vi.490; *bc*, 30) and of mix-up (*Verwechselung*) (vi.491; *bc*, 31), where we find what Benjamin calls the "topographical tradition [of the city of Berlin] that presents [*darstellt*] the connecting [*Verbindung*] with the dead of this ground" (vi.489; *bc*, 28–29). We have only begun to explore this topography, filled less with people than with their names, less with things than with their images. It is to the second half of the nineteenth century, Benjamin or someone writes, "that the following images [*Bilder*] belong, not in the manner of general images, but rather those that according to the doctrine of Epicurus constantly separate themselves out of things and condition [*bedingen*] our perception [*Wahrnehmung*] of them" (vi.489; *bc*, 29).[18] Those images that make up the *Berlin Chronicle* are no more "thing" than they are the stuff of which life is made (vi.488; *bc*, 28). Yet the inevitable mix-up of the object of our perception is such in the grammatically uncertain phrasing above that these images might determine our perception of *either* the image or the thing. Moreover, lost in the translation is another turn of phrase. Literally rendered: "those [images] that . . . separate themselves out of things [*Dingen*] also 'be-thing' [*bedingen*] our perception of them." That the image in its disconnection might create the (illusion of) thing and even be taken for it is the pervasive possibility of mistaken identity and of the fragility of our perception. Perhaps this is why in "Doctrine of the Similar" we read the startling suggestion that it is what is meant [*das Bedeutete*] that gives the name; that "the letter *beth* has the name of a house" (ii.1.208; *ds*, 67).

All this is in the name of a tradition Benjamin calls topographical (in ironic relief, no doubt, to the bio-graphical), the space of Berlin replacing once again the life of Benjamin, the *Schauplatz* replacing the human. But Benjamin's topography, as it connects to the dead, is hardly a question of mapping a surface; rather, it is a displacement and upheaval of that surface in search of one's past. The passage that explores that search claims to define the relation of memory [*Gedächtnis*] to the past, *the* issue of autobiography: it is a treasure, then, in this labyrinthian text where nothing has proven more disorienting than locating its point of departure. That relationship of memory to the past, we read, is unmistakably signified by language: "Language has signified [it] in a way that cannot be misunderstood" (vi.486; *bc*, 25).

And yet, as the passage continues, its language becomes so involved that although one readily understands what Benjamin is getting at, one is still at a loss to know how to follow.

> Language has signified in a way that cannot be misunderstood
> that remembrance [*Gedächtnis*] is not an instrument for the
> gathering of information about the past, but rather its theater
> [*Schauplatz*]. [Remembrance] is the medium of what has been
> experienced, as the earth [*Erdreich*] is the medium in which dead
> cities lie buried in debris. Whoever endeavors to approach his
> own buried [*verschütteten*] past [*Vergangenheit*] must act like a
> man who digs. That determines the tone, the bearing of true
> memories [*Erinnerungen*]. (vi.486; BC, 25–26)

If it is language that has signified unmistakably that memory is the
arena for exploration of the past, rather than an instrumental means to
the past as a graspable end, this is because language and remembrance,
while not identical, often tend to share the same turf.[19] As in the reference to Epicurus, it is a question of bringing forth an image that has a
precarious relationship to the thing, and we will never keep straight
here the difference between the images in Benjamin's text on the one
hand and those he proposes digging out of his past on the other. Benjamin's buried past is like the interred ruins of a dead city. And if his
faculty of remembrance often is less an excavating spade than one that
buries, individual memories also have the power, it would seem, to
disinter: "That determines the tone, the bearing of true memories
[*Erinnerungen*]. They must not shun coming back over and over to one
and the same matter—to scatter it around, turn it up as one turns up the
ground. For [such] matters are only deposits, strata that yield only to
the most careful investigation what constitutes the true worth that lies
hidden within the earth" (vi.486; BC, 26).

And what are these treasures that give themselves only to that per-
sistent return to the same, which at the same time disperses precisely
what it explores? How are we to imagine this strange "mine" of Benjamin, if I may be permitted the play on words? What constitutes the
"true worth" are "the images that, broken loose from all earlier associa-
tions, stand as valuables in the sober rooms of our late insight, like ruins
or torsos in the gallery of the collector" (vi.486; BC, 26).[20] We come back
to the question of Epicurus's images—disconnected from their things,
perhaps victim of the hand of an overzealous archaeologist who brings
forth the work of art, but only as a ruin.

In a sense, Benjamin has told us in the most unmistakable manner just how to view the matter at hand. What we find is severed from its context and in itself broken—an artifact of the human figure destined to become object in a world of art rather than of biography. And yet, if we can find our way back to the beginning, a context is woven from which, it would seem, nothing can ever extricate itself: the insistence on medium and the return to the same, the layerings and deposits with which we are to strew the earth about as we engage in a performance that renders unintelligible the difference between digging up and burying. As we dig about in the past, we indeed seem to inter it, and not only because that which is found is not what was. Language has told us that remembrance cannot unearth the past but can only serve as its place to be viewed [*Schauplatz*]. Benjamin's passage transforms in a layering of similes and images that tell us nothing of the author's past, but everything of the scene of finding it. Remembrance becomes so like the earth in which dead cities are buried (once again turning any fixed relationship between Berlin and the human realm on its head) that she who is in search of lost time must bear herself like one who works, not with pen, but with spade in hand. And she must content herself with that which can be spoken of only as resembling the ruins of someone else's era. The *Chronicle*'s linguistic performance, then, carries out both the archaeological dig and self-burial through a maze of rhetorical figures that leaves nothing as it was.

But, then again, Benjamin admonishes us about what should be written down in all this: "The careful, probing cut of the spade into the dark earth is indispensable and he deceives himself out of the best who preserves in what he writes down only the inventory of the find and not also this dark good fortune [*Glück*] of the place and spot of the finding itself" (vi.486–87; *bc*, 26). The finding, then, must enter what he writes down, not simply that which is found: but, we must not forget, also the failure to find that slides to replace its success: "Futile searching belongs there as much as the fortunate [searching] and therefore memory must not proceed narrating, all the less reporting, but rather, in the strictest sense, epically and rhapsodically to try its cut of the spade in ever different places, searching in ever deeper strata [*Schichten*] in the old ones" (vi.487; *bc*, 26).

All this, it would seem, is an image for the manner in which the past must and must not be told—neither as conventional flowing narrative nor, certainly, as report, but as epic and rhapsody, literary forms that mark their own ruptures.²¹ The passage breaks off here, and yet we have not finished exploring in Benjamin's mine, where, following his directions, we must dig at once in a different spot and yet dig even deeper in the old one. No doubt, it will seem I cheat myself of the point when I choose an earlier moment apparently for its "find," the thematic appearance of an actual mine. Something of a relief after the rhetorical layerings of the later imagery, this passage is a narrative, or perhaps even a report, of his boyhood visits to his aunt. And if *Berlin Chronicle* did not hide both Proust and Benjamin's Proust essay at every turn (most clearly articulated where the French author is *not* mentioned), the visit to Benjamin's aunt might seem to be the real thing—even though it opens with a simile and with a fairy tale.

When the mine appears, it comes forth as the real thing, placed right before the eyes of the careful observer, a real thing, and yet, let us not forget it, a toy, or, as *Berlin Childhood* phrases it: a "toy—if one may call it that" (iv.1.249). This could not escape the notice of Benjamin, the assiduous collector in later life—not of archaeological fragments, but of toys. It is a real thing, then, but also a thing for play [*Spiel-zeug*]: a miniature (as the passages of *Berlin Chronicle* and *Berlin Childhood* have so often been called), an image of the real thing, or perhaps of the mine of images some pages later in the text—of Benjamin's mine of images (constituted of images and designed to mine them, itself the image of remembrance), and yet presented as the real thing. Still, what's the difference? It's all Benjamin's *mine*. For this passage will tell us, perhaps more than any other, how to think Benjamin's past, how to map Berlin, how to read its street signs like the cry of a distant bird in the wood.

> Just as there are for children fairy tales in which a witch or even a fairy rules over an entire wood, so as a child I knew an entire street that a woman had under her sway and that she filled up [*ausfüllte*], although she was always enthroned in her bay window one minute from the house in which I was born: Aunt Lehmann. She was the governor of Steglitz Street. To her room the stairs climbed [*stiegen*] steeply up right behind the hall door; it was dark on them until the door to her room opened and the fragile voice bade a crystalline [*gläserne*] good day and gave the order to put the glass [*gläsern*] rhombus on the table for us that

enclosed the mine in which little men pushed wheelbarrows, toiled with a pickaxe, and shone lanterns into the shafts [*Stollen*] in which transport baskets were always on the move up and down. (vi.472; *bc*, 12)

If the metaphorical mine of the later passage calls on us to recognize, and then forget, the difference between bringing up a find and searching for it in vain, something similar to that takes place here. Though the activities never cease, nothing becomes available beyond the enclosed glass rhombus.

Still, something is always on the move up and down—in and out. No treasure as substance is transported across the threshold between the realm of the toy and the "real" world without. Yet, in the unlit corridors between the two (those that no crack of the door and no lantern can illuminate for us) flit the same valuables that gave themselves up to "the most careful examination" of the probers in the earth (vi.486; *bc*, 26): images broken loose from their former contexts. Just as in Paris the mazes above are mimicked by those below,[22] just as in Paris an underworld labyrinth of tunnels (*Stollen*) connects to and repeats those above, so in the hermetic realm of Steglitz Street the steep, dark stairway to the apartment is repeated in the shafts of the miniature. If a simile sets Aunt Lehmann as the fairy who rules over an entire wood,[23] in a later passage the connection is made to the treasure that lies in her province ("The treasure-keeper . . . in the green pine forest . . . the fairy who grants one wish" [vi.494; *bc*, 34]). Moreover, like the toy she owns, Aunt Lehmann, too, is enclosed by a glass rhombus, the bay window in which she sits like a doll, "always under the same black cap and in the same silk dress," bidding her nephew "welcome . . . from the same armchair" (iv.1.248; *bch*, 32).[24]

We have marked some of the similarities but have hardly fathomed the non-sensuous connection between the toy mine and its apparently real surroundings—a connection that, especially in English, remains all too transparent. It is the voice of the aunt: ordering forth the "glass [*gläsernen*] rhombus," astonishingly a "breakable" voice that itself speaks "*gläsern*"—in a glasslike manner—and whose uncertain, crystalline quality thereby shatters any protective sense of glass that window or toy case might have offered. The apartment with its staircase and the mine, the bay window and the glass rhombus: these are no parallel worlds, separate and contained, but rather realms evoking one another through a certain voice whose frangibility places them on the line.

Aunt Lehmann is here conjured into brief existence: ghostlike, she rises up in the window like a genius loci—filling, we are told, the whole quarter (coincidentally that of Benjamin's birth) with her name, a name and a voice that will prove to be indistinguishable. Are we at last to understand how the names of the dead fill the memorial stones over their graves (VI, 489; BC, 28) even though this is not quite what takes place? Aunt Lehmann "fills up an entire street"—she is the "place holder" (*Statthälterin*) of Steglitz Street: her rule is a question of name, and yet—in what name does that rule take place, and is her name a question of rule?

In the parallel passage in *Berlin Childhood*, "her good North German name vouched [*bürgte*] for her right to hold, for a lifetime, the bay window under which Steglitz runs into Genthiner Street" (IV.1.248; BCh, 32). Yet one wonders if that name could possibly be "Lehmann"—which in German designates its bearer as vassal to another's land and hardly as an enthroned ruler who might rule in her own name.[25] If Benjamin's aunt fills and governs an entire street, it is with a name that is and is not quite hers—one with all the crystalline fragility already ascribed to her voice. Both woman and street have their names transformed through similarities we have yet to trace:

> Because of this aunt and her mine, Steglitz Street could now never again for me be named after Steglitz. A goldfinch [*Stieglitz*] in its cage had more similarity with this street in which the aunt was lodged [*hausen*] in her bay window than the Berlin suburb, which said nothing to me. Where it runs into Genthiner it may be counted among those that remained the most untouched by the changes of the last thirty years." (VI.472; BC, 12)

Only that, *Berlin Childhood* continues, "during this period of time the veil that covered it for me as a child fell" (IV.1.248; BCh, 32), that is, the veil of its acquired name.

What is it, then, that does speak to Benjamin? In this quarter in which the aunt is lodged, both street and relative are invaded by a certain "I." Because of his childhood experience, the street does not take its name from the suburb of Steglitz, is not bound to place or direction as such designations are wont to be.[26] But then again, left and right had not become visceral for Benjamin, who hadn't learned to read a map or to understand his own ineptitude. What says something to Benjamin, rather, is *Stieglitz*, "goldfinch" in English, the vocal creature that the aunt must resemble, sitting in her window like a bird in its cage.

And yet—and this is what makes the passage so difficult to grasp, so like the figures of a half-forgotten dream—if the aunt holds the place of *Steglitz* as *Stieglitz*, giving up her family name (Lehmann), teaching us to disarticulate the street sign in the name of the cry of a certain bird, this is not because of what one thinks one sees, as through a glass clearly—not because, or not exclusively because, the aunt is like the goldfinch. For it is not precisely aunt and bird that are the terms of the comparisons: "A *goldfinch* [*Stieglitz*] in its cage had more similarity with *this street* in which the aunt was lodged in her bay window" (emphasis mine). If it is Steglitz Street that the *Stieglitz* resembles, the similarity can take place only in language.

The *Stieglitz* whose name, in German at least, seems onomatopoeically derived from the sound of the goldfinch's voice,[27] reverberates its call and name in another sense in the relevant passages—as *Steglitz*, *Stieglitz*, to be sure, but also as those stairs that lead to the flat "eine *Stiege* aufwärts" ("one flight up") (iv.1.249), as "*stiegen* die Stufen" ("climbed the stairs") (vi, 472), in the rule of the aunt over a realm into which she does not descend: "ohne noch je darein herabzu*steigen*" ("still without ever descending there") (iv.1.248), or as the mine workers of the toy, "*Steiger*" ("mine inspectors") (iv.1.249)—which explains why it is the "aunt *and her mine*" (vi.472; bc, 12) that transform the name from *Steglitz*.

How can one fail to sense here a connection to the moment in "Doctrine of the Similar" (1933) where Benjamin asks: "In other words: can sense [*Sinn*] be made to underlie the proposition that Leonhard . . . asserts: 'Every word is—and the entire language is—onomatopoeic'" (ii.1.207; ds, 67). Benjamin insists on the onomatopoeic just when he sets forth the concept of "non-sensuous similarity," forcing the reader to abandon the conventional definition of *onomatopoeia* as an association of language with the natural sound of the object it represents. It is in this manner that we might read the shift from "every word" to "the entire language," because Benjamin rejects *Sinn* as sense perception for another sense of Leonhard's phrase, namely, that the entire language is onomatopoeic with respect to itself. Perhaps we are to read the term "onomatopoeic" literally, as a making of the name. Language makes itself, each instant anew, leaving behind the kind of sensuous similarity of *Stieglitz* in its etymological derivation from the sound of the bird's call. Language leaves behind this sensuous similarity for the chorus of reverberations among terms that have no sensual link to the sounds of the objects they may seem to name. Werner Hamacher has said something similar as he works out with exceptional acuity the relations among *Berlin Childhood*, "Doctrine of the Similar," "On the Mimetic Capacity," and "The Task of the Translator."[28]

If the question becomes, both in "Doctrine of the Similar" and in Hamacher's essay, a question of translation, we might go on to say that for Benjamin, all languages are onomatopoeic also with respect to one another; and this has everything to do with his notion of translation. From the very early essay "On Language as Such and on the Language of Man" (1916) a radical concept of translation is already at play *within* the act of naming, a hint of Babel and therefore of a fall, before the Fall, so to speak (II.1.150–51; OLaS, 325).

Thus, language signifies in a way that cannot be misunderstood—but neither can it be understood—that remembrance is not an instrument for gathering information about the past, but rather the medium and theater in which it is embedded and performed. The past is articulated in a glasslike voice—at once window or enclosure and yet brittle and cracking, threatening to shatter itself and its object, and our view of it as well. It is nothing and no-thing: images severed from their context, genealogical trees that speak of familial relations and those of neighborhood, and always of mistaken identities. Thus, in *Berlin Childhood*, there too, the city had woven a veil [*Schleier*] (IV.1.248) in the name of *Stieglitz*.

> The bird Stieglitz gave her the name. And was the aunt not lodged in her aviary like a bird that can speak? Whenever I entered it, it was filled [*erfüllt*] with the twittering of this small black bird who had flown away across all the nests and farmsteads of Brandenburg, where the clan once had its scattered seat, who held both names in memory, those of villages and those of the kindred—which so often were exactly the same.

My aunt knew the relationships by marriage, the residences, the strokes of luck, and the misfortunes of all the Schoenflies, Rawitschers, Landsbergs, Lindenheims, and Stargards who had once been situated in Brandenburg or Mecklenburg as cattle or grain merchants. (IV.1.248–49; BCh, 32)

Of course, only in Benjamin can the songbird Stieglitz speak. And what it says is not only *Stieglitz–Steglitz–Steiger–stiegen–Stiege,* but above all, the names. The cage is "filled" [*erfüllt*] by names: thus, the aunt fills both apartment and street beneath, just as tombstones are filled with the names of the dead. Is this, then, where name and thing might ultimately coincide? The aviary is filled with a twittering—so run Benjamin's memories—of both the names of family and the places from which they came, "so often . . . exactly the same."

But in Berlin things are different: "Now her sons and perhaps even her grandsons were settled here in the West End, in streets that bore the names of Prussian generals and often also of the little towns from which they had come. . . . There a cracked and brittle voice bade me glassily good day" (IV.1.249; BCh, 32–33). Place and name, then, are no longer the same. Isn't this Benjamin's point as he continues? What she may have chirped as family history with all the interweavings of family relations (family trees, so to speak, not entirely unlike those her nephew would find himself drawing years later in a Parisian cafe), what she has in memory as the coincidence between place and name, is inevitably for Benjamin their dissolution (just as *Steglitz* and *Lehmann* were never "the same," or were so only when place and name are transformed into *Stieglitz*). Place and name cracked asunder and yet as similar as BE-RL-IN and BE-NJAM-IN, each bearing witness to the other. In Berlin, a broken voice speaks glassily—like the mosaics formed of capriciously broken pieces of glass to which Benjamin compares the thought fragments whose worth is all the more decisive the less they are capable of measuring themselves on a fundamental conception (I.1.208; OGTD, 29).

There in West End, the bay window apartment is a space (IV.1.249; BCh, 33) in which something valuable is protected, perhaps even hidden: "Doubly secured was this bay window apartment, as is appropriate for rooms that have something so valuable to shelter" (IV.1.249; BCh, 33). The thing of value (*Kostbares*) in Aunt Lehmann's room, must we not understand it, too, as the thingified version of images broken loose from their earlier context in Benjamin's metaphorical mine (vi.486–87; bc, 25–26)? The latter's treasure was the images that stand as valuables (*Kostbarkeiten*) in the sober rooms of our late insight (vi.486; bc, 26). Not only the enclosed glass mine, then, is protected and hidden here. For of the elderly servants who worked for his aunts Benjamin tells us: "They shared a treasure [*Schatz*] with their mistresses, even if it consisted of memories kept silent" (iv.1.250; bch, 34). That the treasures of the flat are the silenced memories should not surprise us, for between silence and twittering (as between speaking and twittering) there is, after all, little difference.

So many mines of treasure—and yet a last to which I must return, if only to give a sense of retracing the thread. It is a mine that so resembles the others we must recognize it as next of kin. As in the metaphorical mine of memory, here, too, the things of value are archaeological objects in the gallery of the collector that appear and that threaten in their crucial moment to break apart into fragments. They are figure and image, we are told—above all, images cut in stone that cannot but remind us of the Tiergarten labyrinth and, perhaps, of the first decipherers of Benjamin's text, Steinschneider and Scholem. Once more, a return to Benjamin's mazes, one that follows immediately upon the series of family trees written down in a Paris café and that seems an answer to so many questions that have come before.

And therefore we are tempted to insist that we have indeed found Benjamin's lost page (if not quite Scholem's), for the long passage presents to us, if not the graphic schema (vi.491; bc, 30), at least one elaborate labyrinth of interrelationship—friendship, comradeship, passions, and love affairs in their most vivid and hidden intertwinings. Against the background of the city, the people around Benjamin close together to form a figure: "Against the background of the people who were the closest to me at that time, the world of things contracted to a similarly deep symbol . . . in four rings" (vi.492; bc, 32).

Benjamin and his friends enter the flat of a dealer in antiquities on the "Kupfergraben" (a name that once again suggests the locus of digging), where they admire through glass cases (not unlike that of Aunt Lehmann's mine, no doubt) an array of ancient jewelry. Four rings are chosen that bind together those there—Benjamin, Alfred Cohn, and the latter's fiancée Dorothea J (but also Ernst Schoen, Jula Cohn, Greta Radt, and, perhaps, Benjamin's wife-to-be, Dora). They are bound together in involutions of relationship that are, perhaps, impossible for the reader to grasp, unless, like Benjamin in the Café des Deux Magots, one gives in to the compulsion of drawing the genealogical tree that might explain them:

> Many years were needed before what at that time was in part beginning to unfold in its germ and in part was still dormant emerged into the light of day in its context: the fate by virtue of which she, who stood in the most intimate relation to her brother which by its tenderness filled to the very edge the limits of sisterly love, was to become the girlfriend of her brother's two closest friends—of the recipient of the ring with the head of Pompey and me—to finally find her husband in the brother of the woman who married her own brother as her second husband—and she it was, on the day I am speaking of, who received from me the ring with the Medusa's head. (vi.493–94; bc, 33–34)

And if a graphic schema can be drawn from this, have we not won back, at least in part, the leaf whose loss left Benjamin so inconsolable, reconstructing at least one of his family trees? Benjamin closes the passage by telling us that a few days later he wrote to the recipient of the fourth ring and enclosed a sonnet, a poem that was sent as a commentary on a stone into which was cut "foliage entwining a lyre"—symbol of poetry covered by leaves, covered in turn by Benjamin's leaf, with the poem: "To your finger, to which it confided itself. . . ." At this ellipsis, Benjamin's editors add the explanation "[Broken off]" in brackets (vi.494; bc, 34). It seems the page with the sonnet has been lost. And how could it be otherwise? That we are bound to lose a page is inevitable, even and especially when we think we can pen it ourselves.

No doubt this is something of what is implicit in the description of the ring Benjamin had chosen. It returns us to the Tiergarten and to the magic strokes of its water writing and to those other figures cut in stone, to the question of the Medusa and to the plea of Benjamin's reader for "biographical information" or "at least . . . [his] autograph" in the letter from Gershom Scholem that opened this chapter.[29]

> It was the most fascinating ring I had ever seen. In a dark solid garnet it presented [*darstellte*] a Medusa head. . . . Worn on the

finger, the ring seemed simply the most perfect of signet-rings. Only he entered into its secret who took it off and then contemplated himself [*sic*] with the head against the light. Since the various strata of the garnet were variously translucent, the thinnest, however, so transparent that it glowed with rose hues, one thought one saw the somber bodies of snakes of the head rise up above the brow under which two deep glowing eyes looked out from a face that with purple-black sides of the cheeks receded once more into the night. Later I tried several times to seal with this stone; it showed itself to be easy to crack and in need of greatest protection. A short time after I gave it, I broke off my relationship with its new owner. (VI.493; BC, 33)

A certain insight is offered here with the power of an illumination. Perhaps this, after all, is Benjamin's answer to the letter with which I opened. Perhaps the labyrinths of which (and in which) he writes, like the snakes of the Medusa head, are always moving. The skill of the gem cutter is such that only when one removes the ring and holds it to the light does one begin to understand. Benjamin is fixed by the glowing eyes of the Medusa in a gesture he insists on calling *self-contemplation*.[30] No doubt Benjamin tried to write, and if not to autograph, then to sign his letters with the ring that appeared, on the finger at least, to be the most perfect instrument for the purpose. But like the voice of his aunt, like the fragment from the metaphorical mine, it threatened to crack, and so he was forced to concede that its secret lay in distancing it from himself, in an act of mirroring contemplation. No doubt this is why, instead of his signature, he wrote the *Berlin Chronicle*.

Three

Walter Benjamin

Image of Proust

> The dialectical image is one that flashes. Thus, as an image that flashes
> in the now of recognizability [*Erkennbarkeit*] is the image of that which
> has been . . . to be held fast. The recovery [*Rettung*] that is accomplished
> in this manner and only in this manner always lets itself be won only as
> the perception [*Wahrnehmung*] of that which irretrievably [*unrettbar*]
> loses itself.
>
> —"Zentralpark," 1.2.682

The journalistic prose of Walter Benjamin's essay "Towards the Image of
Proust" ["Zum Bilde Prousts"] presents the uninitiated reader with a
deceptive code, for in many places it is Benjamin himself who makes it
easy to view his work from the comfortable perspective of conventionally biographical yet undisciplined literary chitchat. One thread of
the argument entangles another, creating an uneven texture of bewildering self-contradiction—as though Benjamin had covered the mar-
gins of his galley proofs with critical self-commentary, but the typeset-
ters, too weary to reset the original text, merely added the new to that
which it superseded.

Read as the straightforward discursive text it pretends to be, the
essay falls short of the demands currently made on literary criticism. It
presents itself as a loose succession of biographical anecdote and casual
commentary that attempts to penetrate "to the heart of the Proustian
world" (II.1.320; IP, 211)[1] by giving the reader apparent access, through
the literary work, to the society, the philosophical thought, and the
author behind the text. Yet the repeated contradiction and discrepancy
that arise from these attempts at penetration offer no sure key to the

mastery of Proust's work, and the hermeneutic rigor which the reader of criticism has come to expect remains conspicuously lacking.

It would be reassuring to attribute this looseness to a blindness of the text to its own self-contradiction. Yet if one writes oneself into the logic of Benjamin's metaphorical web, the text itself accounts for the discrepancies that seem to unfold. The theoretical statement that arises out of such a reading, as oblique and self-negating as it may have to be, may violate the conventional notions of the literary text, the critical text, and the basis for their distinction, but violates them with rigor. Benjamin, like others before him, dissolves an old genre (literary criticism) in order to found a new genre that combines fiction and commentary in one.

Benjamin signals the difficulties of writing oneself into his logic. At the beginning of part II of the essay, in what seems like a casual observation about everyday life, he writes: "The most important thing one has to say is not always proclaimed aloud. And even secretly it is not always confided to those most intimate and closest to us" (II.1.314; IP, 205). This reflection on life serves also as an indication for the interpretation of Benjamin's own text: it does not always say openly what it has to say, not even to the person closest to it, the reader of the text.

One already senses this opaqueness in the title, "Zum Bilde Prousts" (literally translated, "Towards the Image of Proust")[2] Does the essay present a portrait of the man Proust or is it, rather, a discussion of the literary image, a consideration of the Proustian metaphor? Benjamin's text authorizes no clear choice. On the one hand, it speaks of Proust's life, his desire for happiness, his homesickness, his curiosity, his relationship to society, his death. On the other, it speaks of the writing of Proust's "woven" text, of his "cult of resemblance," or of the articulation of his sentences. The biographical portrait is so interwoven with textual considerations about the imagery that no single interpretation of the title seems unambiguously privileged.

Benjamin gives an explicit definition of the term *image,* but it appears in a code language that cannot be learned, except (perhaps) in the course of his essay: "The image [*Bild*] of Proust is the highest physiognomic expression that the incessantly growing discrepancy between poetry and life was able to produce" (II.1.311; IP, 202). In Benjamin's definition the image is neither the image of life nor the image of poetry, but rather, that which marks the ever-increasing discrepancy between the two. "This is the moral," Benjamin continues, "which justifies the attempt to call it [the image] up" (II.1.311; IP, 202). And the essay "Zum Bilde Prousts" is just this attempt—to call up the image, much as one would call an actor before the stage-curtain in the attempt to distinguish him, if only for a moment, from his former fictitious role.

The ambiguous relationship between life and poetry, which underlies the definition of the Proustian image, becomes the fundamental if veiled concern of the entire essay. What is ultimately thematized by virtue of the imposed discrepant interpretations of the term *Bild* is neither Proust's life nor his literary imagery, but rather, the relationship between life and image and what this relation implies about the possibility of interpretative judgment.

Benjamin refers to Proust's image as an expression of discrepancy between life and poetry; and immediately following this description, he begins to elaborate this relationship. In an intricate, repeatedly self-questioning paragraph that attempts to characterize Proust's *A la Recherche du temps perdu,* Benjamin traces a movement between these two extremes, a movement that begins in life and finally leads to the purely ornamental work of poetry. These characterizations involve a particular concept of life and memory in which life seems to assert an original priority over the fictional text and in which memory serves as an access to that life. But each new sentence progressively distances itself from this concept, until life and memory are replaced by a woven (textual) work of forgetting.

> It is known that Proust did not describe a life as it was in his work, but rather a life in the way that he who experienced it remembers this life. And yet even that is still imprecise and far too clumsily said. For here it is not what he experienced that plays the main role for the remembering author, but rather the weaving of his remembrance [*Erinnerung*], the Penelope work of memory [*Eingedenken*]. Or shouldn't one rather speak of a Penelope work of forgetting? Isn't the involuntary memory, Proust's *mémoire involontaire,* much closer to forgetting than to that which is usually called remembrance? (II.1.311; IP, 202)

Benjamin begins in the sure tone of one who is well beyond obvious mystifications about the nature of this "autobiographical work" (II.1.310; IP, 201). It is common knowledge that Proust relates life as he remembers it and not life as it really was. Yet the tone of surety rapidly gives way: Benjamin shuttles back and forth between possibilities, and each new attempt at characterization puts its predecessor into question. The novel is not memory of lived experience, but rather the interweavings of memory, a "Penelope work of memory." Life no longer plays a role here, although the notion of memory still echoes a fragile link to experience. But Benjamin promptly breaks this link: Proust's novel would more aptly be called a "Penelope work of forgetting." The passage begins by describing the literary work as the plenitude of life to which memory gives access, but its final description is the farthest possible from life and memory—the woven work of voided life, forgetting.

As the paragraph continues, it is as though the trajectory from memory of life to the woven poetical text of forgetting cannot be quite completed, as though in describing the literary work one is forced to fall back upon a description into which life once again enters. "And isn't this work of spontaneous memory, in which remembrance is the woof and forgetting the warp, rather a counterpart to the work of Penelope than its likeness? For here the day unravels what the night wove. Every morning, awakened, we hold in our hands, mostly weakly and loosely, only by a couple of fringes, the tapestry of lived experience, as forgetting wove it in us" (II.1.311; IP, 202). Instead of a "Penelope work of forgetting" in which memory has no place, we have an interweaving of the two. Memory directs itself toward an attainable end (it is "goal-linked") and belongs to the daytime of lived experience, to the goal-bound actions of life. Forgetting, on the other hand, unlinked to any goal, is purely "ornament": it belongs to the night in which the patterned carpet of what seems to be lived experience is woven. The interplay between them is such that the life-linked utilitarian memory seems repeatedly to unravel the textured ornamentation that forgetting has woven. "Each day, with its goal-bound action and, even more, with its goal-linked remembering, unravels the weaving, the ornaments of forgetting" (II.1.311; IP, 202).

Yet by the end of the passage, day finally becomes transformed to night, and with it the apparent priority of memory over image or ornament becomes reversed: "Therefore, in the end, Proust transformed his days to night, in order, in the darkened room with artificial light, to devote all his hours undisturbed to the work, to allow none of the intertwined arabesques to escape him" (II.1.311; IP, 202). The life-bound remembrance of the daytime gives way to forgetting, to the artificial and purely ornamental work of the night. The second part of the paragraph retraces the movement away from life and memory toward poetry: in the interplay between the apparently privileged "remembrance" and its counterpart, "forgetting," the ornaments of forgetting win out. The passage marks the same discrepancy that earlier defined the image.

These same patterns repeat themselves throughout Benjamin's essay. Where a passage seems to concern Proust's life, one finds in the last analysis a becoming ornament of memory, a becoming metaphor of remembrance. The long paragraph that closes Part I of the essay, for example, speaks of Proust's "elegiac concept of happiness," in which memory provides access to the past and enables identity or coincidence with an origin. Here, one finds "the eternal once-again, the eternal restoration of the original, first happiness. It is . . . this elegiac concept of happiness that transforms existence into a forest preserve of memory for Proust" (II.1.313; IP, 204).

Benjamin suggests that this same desire for a restoration of the past functions not only in Proust's personal life but also in the literary work, where such nostalgic longings seem to be satisfied by that concept of memory so central to the novel, the *mémoire involontaire*. Mémoire involontaire is brought into play by citing Max Unold's commentary on the well-known madeleine passage: in his interpretation Unold emphasizes the complete success of the episode in carrying one from the present moment to a realm of dream. But here a confusing and unsettling disparity becomes evident. The mémoire involontaire that transports the reader away from the present differs entirely from the notion of memory first described as satisfying the elegiac desire for perfect coincidence with a past. While insisting on the dream as the key to an interpretation of Proust, Benjamin describes this dream world as precisely the realm in which coincidence is absent, for things are merely similar here but never identical: "Every synthetic interpretation of Proust must connect to [the dream]. . . . That is Proust's frenetic study, his impassioned cult of similarity. . . . The similarity of one thing to another that we count on, that occupies us while awake, merely plays around the deeper similarity of the dream world in which what takes place never emerges as identical, but rather as similar" (II.1.313–14; IP, 204).

This fundamental disparity that characterizes the dream as a realm devoid of an apparent plenitude is further elaborated in an oddly pedestrian image. To show how this marking of nonidentity takes place, Benjamin offers us a sign (*Wahrzeichen*) of this world, a rolled-up stocking.

> Children know a sign of this world, the stocking, that has the structure of the dreamworld, when, rolled up in the laundry chest, it is at the same time both "pouch" and "bundle" [*Mitgebrachtes*—literally, that which has been brought along]. And just as they cannot sate themselves with transforming both of them, pouch and contents, with a grasp into a third thing— into the stocking . . . (II.1.314; IP, 204–5)

The stocking is rolled up and thus gives the appearance of being filled. It seems to have an attainable contents, the outside of the stocking functioning both as container and as a sign of its contents. But when the children reach into the stocking, just when that which was formerly hidden (merely indicated) is about to become revealed and present, they discover that the stocking contains nothing but its rolled-up self. The apparent contents do not exist; the outside surface only seemed to assure access to a full interior. The rolled-up stocking that functions as a sign of its own fullness is now emptied of its apparent meaning: it has become an empty sign, signifying nothing beyond itself and serving no purpose. It is mere ornament. But the frivolous nature of the sign does not surprise the children. For them the reach into the stocking is a game. They know from the start that the apparent container is empty. It is not their desire for a content which they have difficulty satisfying: they are obsessed, rather, with the goal-less desire to repeat the game of transforming pocket and contents into the stocking.

Benjamin introduces the stocking as a sign for Proust's dream world: in what way, then, is the "structure" of the stocking in the laundry chest also that of the dream world reached by Proust's mémoire involontaire? Spontaneous remembrance at first seems very like that memory that satisfies an elegiac desire for coincidence with past happiness, but it brings us instead to a world of nonidentity. As the children play their game, the rolled-up stocking seems, like the mémoire involontaire, to promise access to a plenitude behind it; but what seemed to function as a container and as a sign for a fullness is found to have always from the first been a mere stocking, an empty sign.

The children's play with the stocking is like a particular gesture of Proust: just as the children cannot satiate their desire to transform the pouch and its contents into the stocking, "so Proust could not get his fill of emptying the dummy, the Self, with a grasp in order over and over to bring in that third thing—the image" (II.1.314; IP, 205). The *Attrappe* (which may be translated as "dummy," "imitation," or "trap") for which Proust reaches seems to signify the hidden presence of the self. But the grasp that should render this contents present only leads to a voiding of the self. The dummy that seemed to promise the plenitude to self was always a mere image, just as the full pouch of the children was always mere stocking. The gesture of Proust, like that of the children, is only a game. His insatiable desire is not the longing for the presence of the self, but rather simply the desire to repeat the movement, to transform the dummy over and over into the empty image.

Because of the structure of the comparisons, the relationship among the dream, the stocking, and Proust's game is perplexing. The stocking is a sign for the dream world, and Proust's gesture is in turn said to be "like" the children's game with the stocking. What relationship, then, is there between the unsuccessful grasp for the self and an act of memory which leads to the dream world of noncoincidence? In this way the quest for the self is described not only in spatial but also in temporal terms, as a returning to and reappropriating of the past. Benjamin follows the movement of *A la Recherche du temps perdu* where Marcel attempts to make a lost self present to him by recapturing past time. The quest for the self can take place only in this futile attempt to render a past self present. Benjamin compares this unsuccessful reappropriation to the emptying of an apparently full sign in the children's game with the stocking. The sign functions as a trap, as a feigned representation of a reality (of life) existing prior to it and serving as its origin; it seems to promise access to that origin but inevitably turns out to be empty. Memory, like language, seems to be the trace of that which existed before and the promise of its reappropriation. But the movement of the mémoire involontaire, like that of the sign, repeatedly marks the impossibility of this reappropriation. That which we call the self was always mere figure, the "trap" which is an apparent imitation but which cannot coincide with a former origin.

What is bewildering in Benjamin's comparisons of the dream world, the stocking, and the dummy is their striking dissimilarities. If the game with the stocking functions as a sign for the dream world, it is not because their similarity is obvious, not because a stocking in a laundry chest is an evident imitation or representation of a dream world. "The stocking," Benjamin writes, "has the structure of the dreamworld." The structure of both the dream world and the stocking is the feigned movement toward coincidence that leads to nonidentity: it is the structure in which that which might seem to imitate successfully demonstrates its own emptiness, its failure to give access to that which it represented. The similarity between the dream world and the stocking (their structure) is that which states the impossibility of their similarity. The relationship established between the dream world and its sign is one of noncorrespondence, of discrepancy. The dream world does not serve as an origin to which its sign, the stocking, gives access. Benjamin calls the stocking a sign, but chooses a term that avoids the connotation of imitation: the stocking is a *Wahrzeichen*, a sign in the sense of a token.

The construction of Benjamin's comparisons becomes somewhat more comprehensible now. The stocking is like the dream world (it serves as its sign), and Proust's game is in turn said simply to be "like" that of the children. Benjamin refuses to specify whether Proust's grasp for the self is an image of the dream world or the dream world itself. He merely lists a series of elements and calls them similar, so that one is never quite sure which is a sign for which, which functions as a source and which as sign. There is merely a repetition without origin, a repetition that is never identity.

After this tangle of complexities, the paragraph seems to return to its original theme. It began with Proust's elegiac desire for a return to former happiness by way of memory. And as Part I of the essay closes, Benjamin writes once again biographically of the novelist's nostalgic desires; and yet this "homesickness" (*Heimweh*) is not quite the elegiac longing that could be stilled by a restoration of the past. It is stilled, rather, by the image that arises out of Proust's pretended grasp for the self: "The image . . . stilled . . . his homesickness. . . . Torn by homesickness, he lay on his bed. Homesickness for the world distorted in the state of similarity" (II.1.314; IP, 205). We now know this world of similarity for which Proust yearned to be a world of nonidentity.[3] Everything that takes place in Proust belongs to this world of noncoincidence in which nothing more (and nothing less) happens than a repeated bringing forth of the image. "Homesickness for the world distorted in the state of similarity in which the true surrealistic face of existence breaks through. To it belongs what takes place in Proust—and how carefully and elegantly it arises. That is, never in isolation, lofty and visionary, but rather heralded and multiply supported, bearing a fragile, precious reality—the image" (II.1.314; IP, 205).[4] Proust's text may seem to grasp back toward life, toward a former self, but it performs this fictional gesture, this game, merely so that the image may emerge, in order to define the image once again by marking the discrepancy between life and the literary text.

This game that Benjamin describes as Proust's is similar to the game that he himself repeatedly plays. Benjamin speaks of Proust in the nostalgic tone of a memoirist wishing to recall a lost acquaintance to life and in turn presents Proust's yearning as though it were an elegiac desire for childhood happiness: he offers these traps, these dummies of both his and Proust's nostalgia for past life in order to empty them, in order to let them emerge as empty sign—so that the image of his own writing may arise out of the discrepancy marked between life and literature. It rises up out of the articulation of Benjamin's sentences.

The path from the fullness of life to the image has become so familiar that its precipitousness no longer shocks us. We have retraced this trajectory five times in the first section of the essay. And it is through this repetition of similar gestures that we may claim comprehension of these passages, even though this understanding was originally based on a definition of the image which itself was apparently nonsensical—at best cryptical: "The image of Proust is the highest physiognomic expression that the incessantly growing discrepancy between poetry and life was able to produce" (II.1.311; IP, 202).

The manner in which interpretation depends on previous parts of the text becomes especially evident in the opening of the essay's third section. The passage is written in a code that can be deciphered and given full meaning only by reflecting on and reappropriating past language and structure. Benjamin describes Proust's notion of eternity with a peculiar spatial terminology: "The eternity that Proust opens to view is intertwined time, not limitless time. His true interest concerns the passage of time in its most real, that is its *space-crossed* figure" (11.1.320; IP, 211, emphasis added).[5] We are given some indication of what this interweaving of time and space might suggest, when a terse parallel construction places remembrance in the role of time and aging in that of space: "The passage of time in its . . . space-crossed figure, . . . nowhere prevails in a more undisguised form than in remembrance, within, and in aging, without" (11.1.320; IP, 211). The figure of time that concerns Proust is time intertwined with space or the interweaving of remembrance and aging.[6]

This passage reminds one of an earlier "intertwining" of remembrance and forgetting:[7] a counterplay arose between the two, in which the weaving of the purely ornamental tapestry of forgetting finally gained ascendancy over goal-bound remembrance. The new terminology that Benjamin now uses is the counterplay between remembrance and aging—and aging will be seen to play a very similar role to forgetting: like forgetting, aging records the image of lived life,[8] and like forgetting, it both gains ascendancy over its opposite and brings forth the ornament or image.

The Proustian concept of time is heralded in a code language, *Schlüsselsprache* (11.1.317; IP, 208), substantially dependent on earlier passages for its decoding. "Following the counterplay between aging and remembrance means penetrating to the heart of the Proustian world, to the universe of intertwining. It is the world in the state of similarity" (11.1.320; IP, 211). Earlier, Benjamin introduced this notion of similarity (*Ähnlichkeit*) and with elaborate care differentiated the everyday concept from similarity as it functions at the heart of Proust's dream world: that which is similar is that which is "never identical." And what takes place in this world of noncoincidence, the earlier passage also describes: to this realm belongs all that takes place in Proust—the bringing forth of the image.[9]

The puzzling formulation about the nature of Proustian eternity draws its meaning from the two passages previously interpreted, because the laws of remembrance are operative even within the confines of the essay. Remembering what took place when Benjamin first described the intertwining of memory and forgetting (here called memory and aging), and how he later showed the image arising from Proust's "world . . . in the state of similarity" (11.1.314; IP, 205), we may expect here in part III once again to experience the marking of discrepancy between life and poetry and the bringing forth of the *Bild* that has been so carefully heralded: "That is the work of the mémoire involontaire, of the rejuvenating force, which is a match for relentless aging. When the past [*das Gewesene*] mirrors itself in the dew-fresh 'instant,' a painful shock of rejuvenation snatches it up once again as incessantly" (II.1.320; IP, 211). The mémoire involontaire, or rejuvenating force, engages in continual and apparently successful counterplay with the relentless process of aging. The past mirrors itself in the present instant, and the recollection of one's youth is played out when the past becomes snatched up with a painful shock: this shock of rejuvenation brings about a reappropriation of the past.

Yet only a few lines later, Benjamin names this very process in which the past mirrors itself in the present not only rejuvenation but also "aging" or "decay" (*Altern*). "Proust performed the monstrous act, of letting the entire world *age* by an entire human life in an instant" (II.1.320; IP, 211, emphasis added). The gesture that would seem to render one a lifetime younger brings loss of life instead: the concentration of past and present which attempts a reappropriation of life (*Verjüngung*) brings about its instantaneous consumption. "Precisely this concentration, in which what otherwise simply wilts and dims consumes itself in a flash, is called rejuvenation [*Verjüngung*]" (II.1.320; IP, 211).

Proust's grasp toward life—the attempt at rejuvenation through memory—brings aging much as in the earlier passages it brought forgetting (II.1.311; IP, 202), the ornament (II.1.311; IP, 202), or Proust's dream world of discrepancy (II.1.314; IP, 204). We have come to expect his playful gesture that results in voided life, yet as Benjamin goes on, he seems to invert his description of the Proustian enterprise. "*A la recherche du temps perdu* is the unending attempt to charge an entire life with the highest presence of mind [*Geistesgegenwart*]. Not reflection [*Reflexion*]—bringing to mind [*Vergegenwärtigung*] is Proust's method" (II.1.320; IP, 211). A terminology of presence apparently replaces that of decay (aging, wilting, dimming, consuming). Proust chooses to render present rather than merely to contemplate. And yet *Reflexion* and *Vergegenwärtigung* each permit another interpretation. Reflection or mirroring serves as the gesture for the renewal of lost fullness of life ("When the past mirrors itself in the dew-fresh 'instant' "), and *Vergegenwärtigung* may also indicate the realizing of an image. Benjamin's formulation may now be read as follows: Not the attempt to reappropriate the past by mirroring it in the present instant—but bringing in the image is Proust's artistic method. This is not to say that Proust simply chooses the image and rejects the attempts to reappropriate past life. His method is to trace the path from reflection to the image. Benjamin carefully places a dash to indicate just this.

Earlier in the passage Benjamin described this same trajectory as passing from reflection (remembrance, rejuvenation) to aging. How, then, can aging and the recording of the image serve interchangeably to mark this end point? Proust "is imbued with the truth that we all have no time to live the true dreams of existence that are allotted to us. That makes us age. Nothing else. The wrinkles and folds in our faces are the recordings [*Eintragungen*] of the great passions, of the vices, the knowledge [*Erkenntnisse*] that called on us—yet we, the masters, were not at home" (ii.1.320–21; ip, 211–12).

Proust understood that none of us has time to live the drama of his or her existence and that it is this incapacity for immediate experience that makes us age. The process of aging dictates the expressions of our physiognomies, etches our image, the wrinkles and folds of the face:[10] aging is the process that brings forth the image and marks the direction of the Proustian endeavor. This image of ourselves, although it records our lived lives, also indicates our absence in the face of that experience. Our passions and vices and even our knowledge come to us when the self is not at home ("yet we, the masters, were not at home" [ii.1.321; ip, 212]). Thus, all remembrance of things past indicates the inevitable absence of the self from itself. As we pass from rejuvenation and re-membrance of life to aging or the image, the "not [being] at home" of the self becomes apparent and we realize the impossibility both of learning and experience (knowledge, passions, vices). Benjamin summarizes this succinctly in the second part of his essay: "Isn't the quintessence of experience [*Erfahrung*] to learn [*erfahren*] how very difficult it is to learn/experience [*erfahren*] many things?" (ii.1.317; ip, 207).

We have finally been able to decipher all the terms of the enigmatic opening of part III. The interweaving of remembrance and aging, the heart of Proust's world as the state of similarity, the shock of rejuvenation which is also aging, and the etching of the physiognomy—all these we seem to have filled with meaning. The attempt to reappropriate the past through memory results in aging rather than rejuvenation. Aging brings forth the portrait-image that marks the impossibility of direct experience or genuine learning. That which once took place is never rendered present to us as unmediated truth, but only as image.

Yet this very message which our interpretation brings forth, dramatizes a certain emptiness in the interpretative method imposed by the essay. In order to give meaning to an obscure and complex web of images, we were forced to re-collect earlier passages in which these terms and structures first appeared. We grasp back toward these (as toward a past life), investing them with the validity of truth, only to find that the message they enable us to construct is that these "original" passages too were always mere metaphor. Interpretation repeatedly returns us to the figurations of its own language.

If we look over the three passages read thus far, we find each relating a different version of the same story—the story of the becoming-image of memory of life. At the outset of each of these passages, memory seems to promise access to experienced life or to the self; it seems to create a continuum in which reflection may bring about a coincidence of past and present. Memory plays this role, however, with no other purpose than to reveal its fictionality, for it inevitably serves as a bridge to the image rather than to life. And yet such theatrics to bring in the image are not entirely arbitrary. The image can never be presented—except as a relationship between particular images. The image, Benjamin writes, is a frail reality (II.1.314; IP, 205) that emerges from the articulation of the Proustian sentences. It emerges out of a relationship which is also a movement—that is, out of the fiction of its own creation from memory, from life, from the self. The image comes forth as this fictional path becomes marked *as* fiction, as the text which points to its origins is shown always to have been image.[11]

Repeating Benjamin's definition of the image, we find that its terms have been rendered less opaque through their relationship to other passages of the essay. "The image [*Bild*] of Proust is the highest physiognomic expression that the incessantly growing discrepancy between poetry and life was able to produce." That discrepancy characterizes the relationship between life and poetry is the recurrent experience of Benjamin's essay. Every time this poetry (for Benjamin's is also a literary text) attempts to speak of (Proust's) life, one finds a transformation into the image. Benjamin repeatedly thematizes this movement of his own

writing—for example in the becoming-stocking of that which seems to
be a pouch filled with a contents or in the becoming-image of Proust's
dummy self. Benjamin's language, which pretends to be memoir language, which seems to speak of life, states the fictionality of its apparent
endeavor by showing the coincidence of poetry and life to be impossible.

The naming of the image as a "physiognomic expression" has become less enigmatic than at first. At first glance, perhaps, nothing seems
less likely to mark a discrepancy between life and that which names it: a
facial expression, being rather the most unequivocal sign of a particular
human existence, seems to place itself definitively at the pole of life. Yet
the physiognomy has served twice in the course of Benjamin's essay as a
metaphor for the image,[12] that is, as a metaphor for the absence or
forgetting of life rather than for its presence. And it is solely by virtue of
this repetition that the reader learns to invert the "meaning" of the
facial expression. Benjamin names the image a "physiognomic expression" because the violence thus done to this expression, which robs it of
its potentiality to provide immediate access to life, is that which all
language has undergone—and is that which defines the image.

Still problematic in the definition is why the discrepancy between
life and poetry is said to be "incessantly increasing." The gap between
life and literary language could be maintained as constant only if the
two poles of the trajectory could be definitively determined. Yet this
proves possible for neither life nor the image. Life is continually experienced as already in the process of being voided. And the "image" that is
named as the other end point of the trajectory can only be regarded as a
metaphor for itself. The image arises out of the discrepancy between life
and the language that names life (whether it be called "ornament,"
"image," or "physiognomy"): the path between the two poles is tra-
versed only at the price of learning that that which the image names is
absent.[13] The very "presence" of the so-called image at the end of the
trajectory indicates the absence of that which it names—itself.[14]

Neither the image nor life is ever rendered present as a definite
terminus.[15] Nevertheless, Proust repeatedly traces (as does Benjamin)
the path between these illusory vanishing points. Each gesture toward
life, each new pose of language as representational, takes place with an
ever-increasing history of similar gestures before it, and therefore with a
growing cognizance of the game-quality of the gesture that widens the
gap between the two elusive poles.

How successful, then, is the critic's attempt to call up the image that Benjamin suggests as the very purpose of his text: "This is the moral that justifies the attempt to call [the image] up" (ii.1.311; iP, 202)? The attempt to call up figural language from the depths of its textual milieu, to isolate it in order to contemplate it as pure image, proves impossible: the image emerges from a movement of discrepancy and never presents itself directly as the object of experience.

If we read a fourth passage—the one which closes the essay—we find that rather than deepening our knowledge of the Proustian world, it merely brings in another version of a now familiar story. The passage elaborates the symbiotic relationship between Proust's fatal illness and his creation. For this suffering affected not only Proust's daily life, but his art as well: "This asthma entered his art" (ii.1.323; iP, 214). Just how this threat of death entered Proust's art, Benjamin goes on to describe. The syntax of Proust's sentences revealed the fear of choking, a choking that could paralyze the rhythm of the breathing that constituted Proust's art: the inhalation of life to reappropriate past memories and the exhalation of memory through reflection on, or writing about, the past: "His syntax imitates rhythmically, step by step, his fear of suffocation. And his ironical, philosophical, didactic reflection is always the breath with which the nightmare of remembrances falls from his bosom. On a larger scale, death, which he incessantly had present to him, and most of all when he wrote, is the menacing crisis" (ii.1.323; iP, 214).

It is by no means clear that Proust's asthma simply entered his writing by threatening the artist with physical death and his work, therefore, with cessation. Benjamin offers an alternative—by way of an offhand comment—to describe the relationship between this threat of death and Proust's art: "This asthma entered his art, *if indeed his art did not create it*" (ii.1.323; iP, 214, emphasis mine). That the threat of death should come from within Proust's own art rather than from the outside, that his text creates the very basis for its own paralysis will be seen to be the only explanation for the passage that follows: "On a larger scale, death, which he incessantly had present to him, and most of all when he wrote, was the menacing crisis. In this way it faced Proust, and long before his malady took on a critical form. However not as a hypochondriac fantasy but rather as a 'réalité nouvelle,' that new reality whose reflection on things and men are the traits of aging" (ii.1.323; iP, 214).

There can be no mistake that death, this "new reality" which turns all reflection into the traits of aging, is, according to Benjamin's own code language, the image.[16] Proust's art has indeed produced the fatal disease: it is the image, Proust's own creation, that threatens to put an end to the apparently unproblematical respiration of Proust's novel. The image, as we have learned from earlier passages, always brings about a voiding of life. This explains how death could have stood facing Proust long before his physical disease became critical and why it was present to him most especially when he wrote. The image threatens the respiration of the text because as the image arises, it proves the fictionality of inhaling life to recapture memory and exhaling memory to form autobiography: the image arises out of a trajectory that denies reflection and memory as the origin of art.

Benjamin proposes to bring his reader to the very heart of this Proustian creation he has just described by means of "physiological stylistics" (II.1.323; IP, 214). Bizarre as this may appear as a critical methodology, the term simply indicates the continuation of the physiological pattern of imagery already established by the passage: Proust's creation was said to take place in the face of death and to bring forth the physiognomy that marks the process of aging, and the workings of the mémoire involontaire were elaborated in terms of breathing. Benjamin continues to describe this Proustian memory as a kind of respiration. By following this process of respiration we are to arrive at the very core of the Proustian realm—presumably the original reality from which his text arose—and yet the path to this center proves somewhat encumbered: "Physiological stylistics would lead us to the innermost center of this creation. Thus no one who knows the peculiar tenacity with which remembrances are preserved in the sense of smell (by no means smells in remembrances) will be able to explain Proust's sensitivity to smells as accidental" (II.1.323; IP, 214). The conventional notion of Proust's mémoire involontaire points to memory as that which preserves and gives access to the very reality from which the novel was elaborated: yet, according to Benjamin, it does not retain the scents of experience, does not store actual bits of the past. These memories can hardly be the life-source of Proust's work, since they appear as that which has already become image—as physiognomies whose state of presence remains enigmatic if not incomprehensible: "Certainly most of the remembrances we search for pass before us as physiognomies [*Gesichtsbilder*]. And even the free-floating images [*Gebilde*] of the mémoire involontaire are still for the most part isolated, only enigmatically present, physiognomies [*Gesichtsbilder*]" (II.1.323; IP, 214).

And precisely because these memories are already images, in order to penetrate to that which we may name the very deepest layer of Proust's poetry, we must (all the while knowing that it is a mere game) suggest to ourselves a time when memory was not yet image.

> But precisely because of this, in order to knowingly give oneself to the innermost leap [*Schwingen*] in this poetry, one must shift into a special, deepest stratum of this involuntary memory in which the moments of remembrance—no longer singly, as images [*Bilder*], but rather void of images [*bildlos*] and formlessly, indeterminately and weightily—proclaim themselves to us just as the weight of the net announces his catch to the fisherman.
> (II.1.323; IP, 214)

Whoever fishes in the sea of "lost time" in order to recapture past life stages this fiction of life-filled, pre-image depths into which a net might be cast. And as this catch is raised to the surface, it is only by way of language ("his sentences") that it can be brought in—as images rather than life. What Proust brings forth through the mémoire involontaire arises out of the articulation of his sentences, out of that which is already image. "Smell, that is the sense of heaviness of he who throws out his nets in the sea of the *temps perdu*. And his sentences are the whole play of muscle of the intelligible body, contain the whole, the unspeakable strain to lift this catch" (II.1.323–24; IP, 214).

Once again the text plays the game (*Muskelspiel*) of reaching for life through the mémoire involontaire in order to bring in the image. The catch that the sense of smell heralds is not the newly inhaled scents of experience, but memories that were already images. No life-preserving function of respiration takes place here, except that which the literary text itself creates as the image of its own imageless, nonfigural origin.

Benjamin ends his essay with just such a fiction of a moment when Proust's memories were not yet images. He describes the creation of Proust's novel in an ironical arabesque that masks itself as an apotheosis of art. "For the second time a scaffolding arose like Michelangelo's on which the artist, his head crooked backward, painted the Creation on the ceiling of the Sistine Chapel—the sickbed on which Marcel Proust devoted innumerable pages, that he covered in the air with his writing, to the creation of his microcosm" (II.1.324; IP, 215).[17] Proust's deathbed served, as did Michelangelo's scaffolding in the Sistine Chapel, as the uncomfortable structure on which, in spite of great suffering—and perhaps because of it—a momentous work was dedicated to the creation of life, to the origin of the world.

Benjamin may here extol the heroic dimensions of the Proustian creation, but this glorification follows immediately upon a warning against misinterpretation of the relationship between Proust's art and his suffering: "Just how intimate this symbiosis between this particular creation and this particular suffering was, is shown most clearly by the fact that in Proust that heroic Nevertheless with which creative men otherwise raise themselves up [*sich aufheben*] against their suffering never bursts forth" (II.1.324; IP, 214–15). And another such warning appeared earlier in the essay: "Proust himself made it easy for [his readers] in many places to regard even this oeuvre in the long standing, comfortable perspective of renunciation, heroism, asceticism" (II.1.313; IP, 204). The relationship between Proust's creation and his suffering is not literature arising from a melodramatic "Nevertheless" in the face of extreme suffering. Proust's writings did not result from this life condition; rather, it was his writings that created that condition, thus producing the deadly disease that voids life and renders it image.

Benjamin says just this in his closing passage, albeit in his usual oblique manner. Our previous readings put the excessive gravity of these lines into its proper ironical perspective. As Proust lay on his sickbed, we know now that it was no unifying life-source he yearned for: he was torn apart by homesickness for a world of nonidentity, for the realm of the image.[18] If this creation took place in the face of death, it took place in the face of the *Bild* (for which death is a metaphor),[19] the image that indicates the fictionality of lived life.

And then again Proust's creation is not quite identical to Michelangelo's paintings of the creation to which it is compared. The Sistine Chapel paintings present the creation of life as the originary moment of the world. But the origin to which Proust's novel refers is not life, but the creation of the novel itself. Proust devoted his pages to "the creation of his microcosm" (II.1.324; IP, 215); that is, the very subject matter of the novel is its own origin. The novel elaborates the fabrication of its own source, in a life preceding the text from which the image pretends to arise: it does this in order to mark this origin as fabrication, in order to show that life was always a textual image. The text does not arise from Proust's heroic life-will in the face of death, for it is the textual image itself that is the source of voided life.

What Benjamin indicates about (Proust's) literary work is its necessary camouflage as referential language. It apparently provides access to life, to a self existing outside and prior to the text: it offers a plenitude of language which provides a link to a realm external to itself. This feint is intrinsic to the text of fiction, to the text that invariably pretends to be that which it is not. But it is through this assumed role as literal language that the literary work indicates its fictionality. Not that language ever directly presents itself as metaphor or image (*Bild*), but it traces the discrepancy between itself and the life it pretends to name: this discrepancy marks the allegoricity of its representational stance.

Just as literary language indicates its own figural nature, so Benjamin's essay camouflages itself as a language of plenitude and in the course of this dissimulation displays its own allegorical nature. "Towards the Image of Proust," in pretending to read Proust's work as signifying a life which preceded it, lies before us like the rolled-up stocking in the laundry basket. Its language stands in relation to its object (Proust's novel, the society, thought, and author behind it), much as Proust's novel apparently did to its object. But as Benjamin's "critical" essay indicates the purely figural nature of the literary text, it also marks the fictionality of its own language. The name "Proust" and the object *A la recherche du temps perdu* are metaphors in the fiction entitled "Towards the Image of Proust." With the same movement that gives rise to the Proustian image, in tracing the discrepancy between poetry and life, Benjamin indicates the relationship between the critical work and its object. The attempt to penetrate to the heart of the Proustian world, to move toward a coincidence with the literary work, is repeatedly followed by a return to the surface, by the marking of the discrepancy between the critical essay and its object. Benjamin's essay points, necessarily, over and over, to the impossibility of its own discursive statement.

The complex strategy of Benjamin's text in its relationship to *A la recherche du temps perdu* is exemplary. Despite the peculiar theatrical gestures by means of which it chooses to speak of Proust, it nonetheless manages to make general commentary on the relationship between critical and literary texts. Most obviously, it presents an ironical commentary on the criticism which, through the literary work, claims to dis-cover the life (biography, society, psychology) that stands behind it. But Benjamin's essay is no less a commentary on criticism that pretends to be above any mystification about the figural nature of language, which directly advances a concept of language as empty sign and develops these conclusions out of a purely intrinsic literary interpretation. For this criticism that claims to announce the eclipse of meaning in the literary text does so while in the same breath admitting that this announcement was already in its literary object. It further risks displaying the emptiness of its own literal pretensions by unavoidably calling attention to the relevance of this theory of nonreferential sign to its own text. This text, for example, adds nothing to Benjamin's. It cannot claim to deconstruct "Towards the Image of Proust" by revealing the essay's blindness to its own self-contradiction, because the obliqueness of Benjamin's self-commentary is built into the text's nature: the language of the essay is fiction, so that our text merely renders discursive that which was shown to be necessarily oblique. If, as Benjamin's essay indicates, a text is forced to comment on its own figurality indirectly, there is no sure way to distinguish between unintentional self-mystification and an intended strategy of self-camouflage. The signs of the literary text not only necessarily offer an apparent plenitude, but repeatedly perform the text's demystifications. Intrinsic criticism is already within the literary work, yet never appears in the language of traditional commentary, but rather as a discrepancy indicated by a language of fiction. There is a necessary disjunction in the voice of the text, an ambivalence that marks the discrepancy between that which it seems to say and that which it does not and therefore can say. The text—though neither discursively nor definitively—traces the movement between full and empty sign.

Four

Benjamin's Tessera

"Myslowitz—Braunschweig—Marseille"

"Myslowitz—Braunschweig—Marseille." This story is not by me (no doubt that goes without saying). Nor is the phrase that follows that title; for the narrator (let us call him Benjamin for want of a better name) opens his story with "This story is not by me" (IV.2.729).[1] Without quotation marks the assertion is evident; ascribed to the narrator it has incalculable consequences. For the question of putting one's signature to a text is not only the preoccupation of the frame but also that of the interior narration.[2] In that inner tale, by far the richer of the two, the proper signature—as we have yet to see—guarantees the authority of the message, but paradoxically guarantees it only insofar as it is other than the name of the author.

How then are we to read Benjamin's denial of authorship? "This story is not by me. Whether or not the painter Eduard Scherlinger, whom I saw for the first and last time on that evening when he told it, was a great storyteller or not—over that I do not wish to explain myself further" (IV.2.729). Eduard Scherlinger, a painter (*Maler*) appears a single time (*Male*) before the narrator's glance, and only for the duration of his story. Whether he is merely a storyteller, or whether his account is true—as true, say, as Benjamin's "Hashish in Marseille" (IV.1.409–16) or as the protocol he wrote to his hashish experience in June of 1928 (VI.579–87)—the narrator refuses to say. What follows, however, does not follow, for if Benjamin claims with certainty that Scherlinger told the story and refuses only to comment on its veracity, why does he explain himself further with the non sequitur "Whether or not the painter Eduard Scherlinger . . . was a great storyteller—over that I do not wish to explain myself further, because in this era the plagiarist always finds a few listeners who will ascribe a story to someone precisely when he explains that it is simply faithfully reproduced" (IV.2.729). At the juncture of the "because" Benjamin concludes a sentence about Scherlinger by suddenly speaking of a figure who can only be himself, thus performing their conflation just as the content would seem to deny it. Benjamin is on the point of faithfully reproducing another's words, and yet it is precisely in light of this claim that the reader will interpret the story as Benjamin's. And yet at the same time, Benjamin's definition of *plagiarism*—a term that conventionally marks the clandestine usurpation of another's authority—has the plagiarist openly ascribing authority to another. Whether Scherlinger is a great storyteller or not, Benjamin refuses to tell. Whether Benjamin is a great storyteller who has chosen to sign Scherlinger's name, or whether he faithfully reproduces the words of another, or whether he claims to do the latter to reverse our ascription and thus to perform an (inverse) act of plagiarism, nothing in the text will say for certain.

"Typical is a continual alternation of dreamlike and waking state, a constant, finally exhausting being thrown back and forth between completely different realms of consciousness; this can ensue in the middle of a sentence" (IV.1.409) Thus writes Ernst Joël in the article on hashish intoxication chosen by Benjamin to preface his essay "Hashish in Marseille." If what Joël writes is true, can we distinguish between the waking state of the narrating Benjamin that seems to introduce "Myslowitz—Braunschweig—Marseille" and the dreamlike state of the hashish eater? (If not, where is their common ground?) For in the middle of Benjamin's sentence "connections become difficult" (IV.1.409), as Joël puts it, and the marker of causality fails to function. All the possible readings that proliferate, however mutually exclusive, are suddenly packed together and piled up with seismic force.

And yet we cannot help knowing that for much of "Myslowitz—Braunschweig—Marseille" what Benjamin faithfully reproduces are his own texts "Marseille," "Hashish in Marseille" (not yet published), and the protocol to the drug experiment of September 29, 1928—citing each of these extensively. If it is "Benjamin," then, who speaks, let us nevertheless remember that of the thousands of names lying around, he chose to slip into the name "Scherlinger." Perhaps he knew no one by that name, or perhaps, in this the painter's "Story of a Hashish Intoxication," so obsessed with names and their transformations, it is precisely with this name, above all, that he was acquainted. For the name "Scherlinger" misses being "Schierlinger" by a hair—or rather by an *i*.[3] And

Schierling, of course, is a poison, in a story that twice speaks of hashish with that metaphor: "I did not approach the poison as a novice (*Neuling*)" (IV.2.732).[4] Indeed not as a Neuling but as a Schierlinger. Scherlinger already has the drug with him:

> It would be a beautiful romantic embellishment, said Scherlinger, smiling, were I to describe now how through an Arab . . . I could have been in some disreputable harbor bar or other of the city—had come by the hashish. But I cannot use this embellishment, for I was perhaps more similar to those Arabs than to the tourists [*Fremden*] whose way leads them into the same bar. At least in the one point that I also had hashish along. (IV.2.732)

Smiling as he speaks, Scherlinger dismisses the need for the conventional narrative embellishment of the Arab, for in ways we have yet to trace he would seem to incorporate the exotic Arab, the source of hashish, the Schierling in the Scherlinger, as he does the discourse of fiction.

If Benjamin speaks in the name of another, writes in the name of the "poison," metaphorical source of the intoxication itself, it is also in the name of that most famous poison of all, hemlock (*Schierling*), a connection one cannot miss in this tale so obsessed not only with eating the drug but also with drinking (first hot chocolate; then wine; then coffee, which threatens to bring him "to the high point of his pleasure," augmenting "like nothing else . . . the effect of the poison" [IV.2.736]). How can we fail to recognize (with a certain smile to be sure) Nietzsche's Socrates, who, as he is about to drink the hemlock and thus to leave behind the Apollonian voice of reason, finally turns to music.[5] For the resonance of music is unmistakable here, from the early description of Scherlinger as *verschollen* ("missing," but also, literally, "he whose sound has died away") to the closing passage of the text.[6]

Although "Marseille," "Hashish in Marseille," and the various drug protocols find their way here, we must renounce their pretensions to serious description, caught as we are in the fold of the name *Scherlinger/Schierling.* Benjamin writes (almost) in the name of the drug, and despite the philosopher's voice that occasions and seems to precede the tale of hashish, it is impossible to miss an already reverberating laughter. "Then my friend, the philosopher Ernst Bloch, let fall a proposition, in some connection or other which I have never learned, that there was no one who had not once in his life already come within a hair of becoming a millionaire. We laughed" (IV.2.729). This is a warning, the inner story tells us: "For it is with . . . laughter . . . that the intoxication begins" (IV.2.734). The proposition of the philosopher loses its context and comes forth as a paradox: the story of the story's telling—perhaps narration in general—is, before the fact, intoxication.

What we might (in complicity with what is to come) call the outskirts of the work, lending to the text, as Benjamin was wont to do elsewhere, a topographical metaphor,[7] are thus in no way irrelevant. The opening paragraph already declares the state of emergency, the decisive if incalculable battles of narrative frame and inner narration, also those of self, name, drug, the overly precipitous chess moves in which royal stakes (and are these not, in chess, the killing of the king?) are never to be secured by strategy.

Scherlinger tells his story. Emotionless, he notes the death of his biological father, whose only significance is the fortune he has left behind (and perhaps the family name). In mid-sentence we find this hastens his departure in the direction of his spiritual father, the nineteenth-century French painter Monticelli, to whom Scherlinger has "everything to thank," if not in his fortune, then in his art (IV.2.729). While in the native city of Monticelli, Scherlinger is called upon to complete the transaction that would multiply the inheritance left behind in Berlin—native city of Benjamin and Scherlinger, that shares with each much of its name (*Be—in, erlin*), origin and would-be destination of the action, locus of the storytelling, the only city omitted from the title.

For the painter has left his finances in the hands of a young bank official who is to contact him in Marseille, should the "possibility of conversion arise" (IV.2.730).

> "You would only have"—thus [the bank officer] concluded—"to leave us a password [*Kennwort*] here." I looked at him devoid of understanding. "We can, namely," he explained, "carry out orders that come by way of telegram only when we protect ourselves, in so doing, against misuse. Assume we wired you and the telegram came into the wrong hands. We protect ourselves against the consequences by agreeing with you on a secret name which you set below your telegraph orders instead of your own."

I understood and was perplexed for a moment. It is still not so simple all at once to slip into a foreign name as into a costume. Thousands upon thousands are lying around ready. . . . How incalculable the choice and how full of consequences. Like a chess player who has gotten himself into a fix and would prefer to leave everything as it was, [who] finally under the necessity of making a move, however, moves a piece, I said: "Braunschweiger." I knew no one with that name, nor even the city from which it takes its writing. (IV.2.730)

Braunschweiger: an inhabitant of the city of Braunschweig, but literally, if broken into its parts (like the pieces of a mosaic), "brown" (*Braun*) and "he who keeps silent" (*Schweiger*). Braunschweiger is a "secret name" to confirm Scherlinger's identity, to guarantee the bank's control as well as the narrator's authority to increase his fortune.

And yet one need not read on to understand that none of this will come to pass as calculated. From the beginning, the story is to fulfill Bloch's proposition: Scherlinger has missed becoming a millionaire. Moreover, he has always understood that his act of naming is less the certification of a *Kennwort* (the bank official's term), a word that promises knowledge and unequivocal recognition, than the choice of a tessera. In Roman times the tessera was a small tablet (as of wood, bone, or ivory) that might be used as a means of identification—though it was also a piece, as of marble or glass destined to be used in mosaic work (OED). (And Marseille's main artery, Scherling tells us, is filled with mountains of glass that simulate the treasure of jewels [IV.2.731].) Let us just say for now that in "Myslowitz—Braunschweig—Marseille" the token of identity has the "possibility of conversion" into the small, if not insignificant, piece of a complex mosaic and all that implies in Benjamin.[8] If the bank official wants the name as *Kennwort,* to regulate the consequences (*Folgen*) and to ensure "in the most certain manner" a calculable increase in Scherlinger's assets, Scherlinger understands that the choice is "incalculable" and "full of consequences" (*folgenschwer*) that cannot be banked on. The move to choose a name, he tells us, comes as an inevitably arbitrary move in a game otherwise governed by strategy, for he chooses "Braunschweiger" like a chess player who has gotten stuck but is nevertheless forced to make a move.[9]

The name, it would seem, means nothing, or at least, there is no strategy behind it and no significance that attaches it to either person or place. A totally unmotivated choice, oxymoronically a will-less decision, among the thousands and thousands he might have uttered. Destined to carry no other meaning, it is intended as the indifferent but certain marker for Scherlinger that assures the stability of a writing across distance (telegraph). Yet how could "Braunschweiger" grant such assurance when within the name—in its hardly inconsequential writing—is the secret name of silence (*Schweigen*)?

Scherlinger arrives in Marseille at noon: he tells first of his afternoon wanderings in pages that plagiarize Benjamin's "Marseille."[10] He turns to his nocturnal encounter with hashish, ending his narration precisely twenty-four hours later. Scherlinger takes the hashish which he has all along had with him, though it seems without effect. He lies in a room of the Hotel Regina (let us keep this name of the sovereign in mind) reading (of course), lost in himself, utterly certain that no one in this vast city of Marseille knows his name. And yet, inexplicably, there is a pounding at his door. The telegraph carrier brings the message "Recommend buying 1000 Royal Dutch Friday first quotation wire agreement" (IV.1.733). The narrator has till midnight to reach the post office and complete the communication by signing the name of another to prove he is himself. The "possibility of conversion" offers itself—bank deposit for "Royal Dutch" and with it, it is understood, the transformation of Scherlinger into a millionaire—unless, of course, he misses that conversion (by a hair), and that in the name of transformations equally but otherwise royal that only the poison can bring about.

For the poison is at work, even (perhaps first and foremost) when we feel its absence, as a continual alternation between fullness and void, consumption and renunciation. Thus, certain that he has consumed the drug to no effect, but wary lest "against all expectation" (IV.2.733) it nevertheless should begin to work, Scherlinger sets out to guard himself against "the all-consuming hunger" (IV.2.733) it produces.

> To buy a bar of chocolate seemed to me advisable in any case. In the distance beckoned a display of candy boxes, mirroring tinfoil, and beautiful pastries piled high. I entered the shop and hesitated. There was no one to be seen. But that struck me less than the completely strange seats, at the sight of which I had to realize, for better or worse, that in Marseille hot chocolate is drunk

on high thronelike seats that most resemble operating chairs. Then from the other end of the street the owner came running over in a white smock and I had just enough time, laughing aloud, to flee his offer to shave me or cut my hair. Now I first realized that the hashish had already begun to do its work long before, and if the transformation of powder boxes into candy boxes, nickel cases into bars of chocolate, wigs into tiered cakes had not apprised me of that, then my own laughter would have been enough warning. . . . Thereupon the demands of time and space made by the hashish eater came into play. They are, as is well known, absolutely sovereign (*königlich*). For the eater of hashish, Versailles is not too big and eternity does not last too long. (IV.2.733–34).

Scherlinger never gets his chocolate in this the first of a series of non-consumptions. And if there is laughter as a warning here, it has something to do with not grasping the scene as a simple "transformation of powder boxes into candy boxes, nickel cases into bars of chocolate," etc. For other transformations take place that both cite past moments and prefigure the future and that cannot be reduced to the circumscribed substitution of delirium for a more sober reality.

On his way to close the sale of Royal Dutch, the narrator, whose demands in terms of time and space take on royal dimensions, is offered a thronelike seat where he might partake of the deep brown liquid that will surface again in a cup of coffee that threatens to intensify his intoxication—a chair on which, he is made to realize, sooner or later one is bound to have one's hair cut, that famous hair by which Scherlinger, we know, will miss bringing a certain communication to pass, a cutting or shave which is already in place, at least partly because of his name.[11]

Under the circumstances how can one keep in sight what it is one wishes to achieve, where one wishes to go, and the limited period of time in which one has to do it, all the while maintaining that "wonderful sense of humor" that questions "all that exists" (IV.2.734). Scherlinger finds the Marseille post office and finds it in time—its illuminated clock gleaming from its tympanum. But if you can have your hashish and eat it too in this story, that is not the case with anything else and certainly not with the locus of communication. "In front of [the post office] I could not turn my glance away, indeed I felt how much would have escaped me had I drawn too near to it and thus lost the whole thing from sight and above all the gleaming moon clock" (IV.2.734).

While not losing sight of the post office, which was "prepared . . . to take in and pass on the invaluable understanding" (IV.2.734) and thus transform Scherlinger into a millionaire, Scherlinger finds that the hashish has turned him into something else: "Namely, it allowed me to become a physiognomist" (IV.2.735). Namely and not so namely, for although in every new countenance an old acquaintance seems to arise, "often [Scherlinger] knew his name, often not" (IV.2.735). Seated in a cafe of questionable repute, once again failing to consume the drink before him, preferring to hang on the image that inhabits it (IV.2.736), as he contemplates the faces around him the artist discovers another form of wealth: "I grasped now suddenly how for a painter—did it not happen to Leonardo and many others?—ugliness could appear as the true reservoir of beauty, or rather the receptacle of its treasure, as the ruptured mountain with the entire interior gold of the beautiful that flashed out of folds [*Falten*], glances [*Blicke*], and features [*Zügen*]" (IV.2.735).

"When we have eaten hashish we know nothing of ugliness" (IV.2.734). But what do we know of beauty? For the artist—namely Leonardo, Rembrandt,[12] Monticelli, Scherlinger, Schierling—ugliness might appear as the locus of a treasure which, while not destined to turn him into a man of monetary wealth, still, like the gold inside a mountain, might gleam from the features and folds (*Falten*) of the face if one only knew the open sesame, the password that might give us access.

And yet, when Scherlinger speaks of the face he most remembers, the gold that gleams from the physiognomic wrinkles appears by another name. "I especially remember a boundlessly bestial, common male face from which suddenly the 'Fold [*Falte*] of renunciation' violently struck me" (IV.2.735). In the face folded in upon itself, the gold of beauty (if we may call it that) is resignation or renunciation, as indeed the gold of all artistic beauty may be for Benjamin.[13] The transformation of ugliness to the beauty that inhabits art is not destined to grant possession. Thus, "Myslowitz—Braunschweig—Marseille" is a tale of constant change without consumption, of fullness that gives way to cutting, always with an inevitable laughter:

My neighbor, however, . . . constantly changed form, expression, fullness of his face. The cut of his hair, black-rimmed glasses made him now severe, now genial. Indeed I said to myself that he could not change so quickly, but that accomplished nothing. And he already had many lives behind him as he suddenly was a secondary-school boy in a small easterly city. He had a pretty, cultivated work room. I asked myself: where does this young man get so much culture from? What would his father be? Draper or grain agent. Suddenly I knew: that is Myslowitz. (IV.2.735–36)

In this passage that finally elucidates the title's third term, one wonders if the neighbor is among those whose name Scherlinger claims to know: "In every new countenance before me an acquaintance appeared; often I knew his name, often not" (IV.2.735). For the countenance in question that changes so quickly, whose fullness of face is never quite the same, and whose "cut of [the] hair" is bound to make us smile, this neighbor who has so many lives behind him is described by Ernst Joël in the protocol to his hashish experiment of May 11, 1928—almost word for word (VI.577): Joël calls him *"Benj[amin]."* Scherlinger seems to call him Myslowitz, although he then shifts that appellation brusquely from the human figure to the square. Here, we might remember Benjamin's early reference to plagiarism, or perhaps, though inversely, what it means to write in the name of another. But above all, we must recall what Scherlinger says of the laughter that accompanies the intoxication, even when it is a question of renunciation. For how can we fail to hear in this author for whom "Glück" maintained such resonance, a joke (*Witz*) about *Mazel* ("Myslo"), the Yiddish word for luck or good fortune: *Myslo-witz.*

It is "Myslowitz," then, the square before him, the scene of so many transformations of face, in which a gymnasium reminiscent of Benjamin's Kaiser Friedrich school appears (in *Berlin Chronicle*, VI.494; BC, 34). Here, the post office might offer the fortune Scherlinger seeks (were it not for the joke the hashish plays), if as an artist he took seriously such things as where he stands and in which city, who he is, who narrates his text, how to envisage his neighbor, or himself, or anyone else who enters the space of Myslo-witz.

> But when I looked once again at the square I saw that it had the
> tendency to change with everyone that entered it, as though it
> were forming a figure for him which, it was well understood, had
> nothing to do with how he saw it but rather with the view which
> the great portrait painters of the seventeenth century, according
> to the character of the person of quality whom they place in
> front of a gallery of columns or a window, throw into relief
> against this gallery, this window. (IV.2.736)

If earlier it is the human physiognomy that alters with inconceivable
rapidity, here it is the space which that form occupies—the background,
it would seem—that has the tendency to change. And yet, in the passage
above, where the translation fixes the meaning in the interest of maintaining a logical perspective, the German original cannot be made to
hold so still. The relation between the square and the human is defined
by a series of interchangeable pronouns that are not to be distinguished
with such certainty. Thus, we might read that the square changes as
though forming a figure that has nothing to do with how the person
sees it, or (equally possible) how it sees him. In the square of Myslowitz
and that of the post office, the human and the architectural, viewer and
viewed, the namer and named (as we have yet to see), are all at loose
ends.

But then again, the figure that is formed has nothing to do with how
either one regards the other, for the dominion of figuration is displaced
to the view of the seventeenth-century portrait painter. Yet in this narration about physiognomies, where we are reminded of the painter's skills,
the "view" of the artist is not his glance—not his powers of seeing—but
Blick, as the distant background (view) thrown into relief against col-
umns or window, against which the human is in turn portrayed.

It is difficult to know who paints this picture that skips from Scherlinger's view of the square to the unstable relation of square and human
form, to the artist's "view" (which is yet not his glance), the distant
background in which both the setting and the human are suddenly
rendered secondary. It is easy to understand that the narrator "[sinks]
completely into this image [in which he] no longer [finds] a ground"
(IV.2.736).

But abruptly, Scherlinger claims, all is "completely clear," and he
knows he must send the telegram. He orders a coffee to stay awake. "A

few finger widths from my lips, however, my hand suddenly stopped—to my own astonishment or out of astonishment—who could know?" (iv.2.736). Whether it is the narrator who is taken aback or whether it is his hand, Scherlinger refuses to say—for self and body part company here. The brown liquid never reaches his lips—and one might well ask whose lips these are. The cup of coffee, too, is not necessarily itself. Taken by the sober "to remain perfectly awake," "for every eater of hashish" "[coffee] augments namely like nothing else the effect of the poison" (iv.2.736).

If the cup does not touch his mouth but "[remains] floating in front of [him] in the void" (iv.2.736), neither waking the lucid nor drugging the intoxicated, how are we to speak of what follows? Is it the triumph of clarity or the "high point" of his high? For Scherlinger in a sense, but then again perhaps not, performs the communication that was to make him rich. Though the telegram is never sent, at least let us say he assumes the name Braunschweiger as never before: "My glance [*Blick*] fell on the folds [*Falten*] cast by my white beach pants, I recognized [*erkannte*] them, folds [*Falten*] of the burnoose, my glance fell on my hand, I recognized [*erkannte*] it, a brown one, Ethiopian . . . " (iv.2.737).

The painter's *Blick* seems finally his own. Engaged in gestures of self-contemplation, however accidental, the artist discovers what will bring him to himself—if not quite to *his* name, then to that he must use in place of his own to assert his identity. But what is it, exactly, that Scherlinger glances? The hand that just before had an independent consciousness ("my hand suddenly stopped—to my own astonishment or out of astonishment") returns in a moment of apparent self-cognition: "I recognized it, a brown one, Ethiopian." The wrinkles of the human visage with its various treasures return as "folds of the burnoose," the hooded cloak of that Arab with whom Scherlinger has already claimed such similarity ("for I was perhaps more similar to these Arabs than to the tourists" [iv.2.732]). If Scherlinger recognizes what seems himself in the fold of the burnoose—have we not been here before?—it is as the source of the drug, the ornate marker of a text's fictionality, as the otherness of the exotic, and also as reservoir of an interior wealth—in which everything points to "brown/Braun."

But that, of course, is only half the story. For while the fold serves metaphorically as receptacle of riches, of the gold within the mountain's stone, beauty hidden in the guise of ugliness, it is also the "fold of renunciation." In a gesture of self-denial that refuses consumption and also speech, neither the coffee in the cup nor the ineluctable name is able to pass the renunciatory fold of the lips compressed upon one another.

> [While] my lips remained austerely closed, adhering to one an-
> other, denying themselves in like manner the drink and the
> word, there rose to them from inside a smiling, a proud, African,
> Sardanapalian smiling, the smiling of a man who is about to see
> through the course of the world and fate and for whom there are
> no more secrets in things and in names. Brown and keeping si-
> lent [*Braun und schweigend*] I saw myself sitting there. *Braun-*
> *schweiger*. (IV.2.737)

Denying themselves both the drink (*Braun*) and the word (*schwei-gen*), what the lips fail to either take in or speak out rises up from within—in the guise of that "intimate . . . laughing" with which, we have already read, "the intoxication begins" (IV.2.734). Begins and appar-ently ends. As never before, Scherlinger is *Braunschweiger*: this is the joke. And Braunschweiger not exactly in name alone. The narrator *is* Braun-schweiger (brown and silent), self and name no longer distin-guished: for the configuration of thing covered by the exterior costume or the stony wall of an indifferent name has been seen through.

If names and things or namer and named come together where the gold of true identity and the fold of renunciation share an uneasy locus, something similar is at stake in "Doctrine of the Similar" when the fig-ure of the astrologer reads the stars. The opening pages of that essay in-sist on linear temporal sequences: on a "history" of man's production of similarities, for example, or on "natural correspondences" that precede and stimulate a response, on an already present similarity that is in turn imitated, and, above all and repeatedly, on an originary state that is fol-lowed by interpretation (II.1.205–6; DS, 65–66). But as Benjamin offers the example of the constellation, we can no longer regard historian or reader as interpreters brought in to confront a lost past. Moreover, no treasure or reward (*Lohn*) is made present to hand (II.1.207; DS, 66). Possession can now only be spoken of in a narrative fiction. Thus, the concept of non-sensuous similarity means "that we in our perception no longer *possess* that which once made it possible to speak of a similarity that exists between a star constellation and a human" (ɪɪ.1.207; ᴅs, 66). For the perception of similarity is suddenly bound to an instantaneous flash;

> The perception [of similarity] is in every case bound to an instantaneous flash. It flits by. . . . It offers itself to the eye just as fleetingly, transitorily as a constellation of stars. The perception of similarities therefore appears bound to a moment of time. It is like the supervention [*Dazukommen*] of the third, of the astrologer, to the conjunction of two stars that wishes to be grasped in the moment. (ɪɪ.1.206–7; ᴅs, 66)

The moment of interpretation, what Benjamin calls the perception of similarities, takes place from no privileged, external vantage point. Rather, the reader-astrologer is taken into the constellation in a flash—perhaps not unlike Scherlinger and Braunschweiger.[14]

Scherlinger's moment of self-contemplation, which is also the moment of giving himself a proper name, takes place as he discovers that words and things no longer have secrets: they are no longer caught in what Benjamin elsewhere calls "the bourgeois conception of language" where language is the means of expressing something else outside it (ɪɪ.1.144; ᴏʟas, 317–18). What Scherlinger speaks of as "recognizing"—or, perhaps more properly translated, "cognizing" (*erkennen*)—plays a critical role in the early essay "On Language as Such and on the Language of Man" in its preoccupation with Adamic naming. There, Benjamin describes God's creation as a linguistic act that begins with "Let there be" and ends with "He named" (ɪɪ.1.148; ᴏʟas, 322). Thus, the language of God is that which creates and that which completes, creative word identical to the name. At the same time God cognizes (the German term is again *erkennen*): there is an "absolute relation of the name to knowledge [*Erkenntnis*]" (ɪɪ.1.148; ᴏʟas, 323). Adam, who is made in the image of God, is in turn assigned the task of a naming to which cognition is also bound (ɪɪ.1.148, 151; ᴏʟas, 323, 325–26). Thus, when Scherlinger cognizes the folds of the burnoose and his own Ethiopian hand, when, *Braun* and *schweigend,* he names himself *Braunschweiger,* all of this is a parodic version of the first man in paradise, here the paradise of the hashish high.[15] Much could be said about the critical differences between Adam and God and between Scherlinger and

Adam, and also about what Benjamin calls "the theory of the proper name" (ii.1.149; olas, 324). For all of these complexities, nevertheless, in "Myslowitz—Braunschweig—Marseille" the connection unmistakably resonates in the reference to Baudelaire's *paradis artificiels*. One might contemplate the ironies of invoking an Edenic mode of language as name through an insistence on artificiality.

Yet in the moment of Adamic cognition and naming, Scherlinger tells us, he is not quite, or at least rather beside, himself. *Braun* and *schweigend*—the narrator sees himself there: for this moment of identity with his name, where names and things no longer have secrets, marks a split of another order. And is this not part of that "wonderful sense of humor" that implies a "boundless dubiousness of all that exists" (iv.2.734)? The closer one looks at a person, especially oneself, the more distantly that person looks back at you.[16]

"The sesame of this name that was supposed to shelter all riches in its interior had opened up" (iv.2.737). The name, like the ruptured mountain, the metaphor of the human visage, was to shelter and conceal all riches within. But it is not the name as receptacle of treasure that opens up here. Rather, the beauty of the phrasing is such that what discloses itself is the *sesame* of this name, the linguistic force of magic that has the power to open the name—a force in which the differentiation between gold and renunciation is a laughing matter.

What *sesame* opens up as well, of course, is "Ali Baba and the Forty Thieves," a tale narrated by that consummate story teller Scheherazade. If I had her linguistic powers I would retell in all its richness the story of "Ali Baba." This story lies like a treasure at the interior of "Myslowitz—Braunschweig—Marseille," and not only because Benjamin utters the magic "Sesame." For in "Ali Baba," too, there is, if not a mountain, at least an imposing rock inside of which a treasure awaits whoever is able to remember the proper word. And it is a tale of two brothers, one wise and one foolish, one abstinent and one greedy (perhaps not unlike Scherlinger and the bank official), whose difference in approaching that fortune is at least one major thrust of the narration. When Ali Baba enters the cave, he fills his sacks with gold by first emptying the thieves' provision sacks. Thus, he spends the consumable food to take in a wealth that he will then rebury in the earth and which he will go on to use, only with greatly measured caution. His brother, Kasim, however, loads up in the cave what it will take ten mules to carry. No bags of grain

are emptied first, sign of a certain renunciation. In front of the impass-
able rock and anxious to leave, forgetting the magic word, Kasim calls
out "Open Barley," the very grain his brother saw the thieves carrying to
the cave. He goes on to name "all the cereals and different varieties of
grain the hand of the Sower threw on the surface of the fields in the
infancy of the world," for Kasim mistakes the sense of the word as object
of appetite and thus loses the magic of its power.[17] The power of *sesame,*
which can be indifferently linked to "open" or "shut," has nothing to do
with a grain one spoons to consume.

Rather, let us say with Benjamin, "With a spoon one must ladle the
similar [*das Gleiche*] out of reality," for "[Scherlinger] was a young man
who had a sense for all that is similar [*Gleichartige*] in the world"
("Hashish in Marseille," IV.1.414; HiM, 142).[18] With a spoon, or with a
cup, or with the gesture that places into one's mouth the hashish that
seems to have no effect at all; consumption with self-denial, the fold in
which both gold and renunciation have their place; a self-recognition in
which one is always beside oneself as other—Braunschweiger, Ethiopian,
Sardanapalus, the Arab of the burnoose. The wealth of "Myslowitz-
Braunschweig-Marseille" is not there to be eaten or possessed but is
rather produced in "a continuum of transformations" (II.1.151; OLaS,
325)—which also are translations—transformations in which identity
and similarity [*das Gleiche*] prove indistinguishable. And this is because
"the closer one looks at a word, the more distantly it looks back at you"
(IV.1.416; HiM, 144). Thus our "insight into the realms of the 'similar' "
has been won here "less by showing similarities already hit upon than
through the reproduction [*Wiedergabe*] of the processes that engender
such similarities" (II.1.204; DS, 65). Such is hashish, reading, and writing.
Much more could be said, yet here I will remain discreetly silent.

We are faced with the incredible if not literal riches that an opened
"sesame" can offer up, for *Braunschweiger* comes into full force only
with the ringing of the midnight hour, only in the moment when the
name is rendered impotent to control the consequences of material
wealth.

> At this point all the church towers of Marseille broke in on me
> like a chorus, festively and confirming with their striking of mid-
> night. . . . I rambled along the bank of the quay and read the
> names of the boats. . . . While doing this an incomprehensible

gaiety overcame me and I smiled successively in the faces of all the girls' names of France—Marguerite, Louise, Renée, Yvonne, Lucile—the love which was promised to these boats with their names seemed to me wondrous, beautiful and touching. Next to the last one stood a stone bench [*Steinbank*]; "Bank," I said to myself and objected that it did not also sign its name on a black background with golden letters. That was the last clear thought that I composed in this night. The midday papers gave me the next one as I woke up in the hot midday sun on a bench on the water. (iv.2.737)

Once again Scherlinger sits—beside himself—as he has from the first suggestion of the barber's thronelike seat, to the cafe in the square of the post office and Myslowitz, to the last seat of all from which he will awaken just twelve hours after the crucial midnight hour. On a *Steinbank*—a "stone bench" if one wishes to make sense of the action, but a bank of stone if one touches on the wondrousness of the noun—once again the stone whose implicit, interior, bankly wealth Scherlinger no longer desires—rather, only its written name, its signature, so to speak (of gold, of course), a transposition of his spoken word ("'Bank,' I said to myself") to the written, which, elsewhere, Benjamin calls the most non-sensuous similarity of all (ii.1.208; ds, 67).

At midday, then, the newspapers announce "Sensational rise in Royal Dutch" (iv.2.737), an announcement in which Scherlinger senses no loss. His mood, rather, echoes those festive bells of midnight that rang the closing of the post office: "Never have I felt, the storyteller [concludes], so resonant [*klingend*], clear, and festive after an intoxication" (iv.2.737). The narrator misses becoming a millionaire, but he experiences, perhaps like no one else, a sensational rise in royal Deutsch.

Five

The Monstrosity of Translation
"The Task of the Translator"

Therein . . . lies the master's real secret of art—that he obliterates the
subject matter through the form.
*Darin . . . besteht das eigentliche Kunstgeheimnis des Meisters, daß er den
Stoff durch die Form vertilgt.*

> —Schiller, cited by Benjamin in
> "Zwei Gedichte von Friedrich
> Hölderlin" (ii.1.125)

In 1923, when Walter Benjamin published his translations of Baudelaire's "Tableaux parisiens," he prefaced them with a short essay entitled
"The Task of the Translator" ("Die Aufgabe des Übersetzers").[1] Was this
essay intended to unfold for us the nature of the difficult task that
claimed so many years of Benjamin's life? Does it signify an unprecedented consideration for the understanding of his readers—for those to
whom the reading of lyric poetry would present difficulties? No less
than the introductory poem of Baudelaire's *Flowers of Evil*, "To the
Reader," the opening lines of Benjamin's essay close the gates abruptly
on such illusions of brotherly concern. "The poem to the reader closes
with the apostrophe: 'Hypocritical reader,—my likeness,—my brother!'"
The situation turns out to be more productive if one reformulates it and
says: "[Benjamin] has written an [essay] . . . that, from the beginning,
had little expectation of an immediate public success" (from "On some
Motifs in Baudelaire" [1.2.607]).[2] "Nowhere does consideration for the
perceiver with respect to a work of art or an art form prove fruitful for
their understanding. . . . For no poem is intended [*gilt*] for the reader,
no image for the beholder, no symphony for the audience" (iv.1.9).

What Benjamin's essay performs (and in this it is exemplary among his works) is an act of translation. It is, to begin with, a translation of "translation," which then rapidly demands an equally violent translation of every term promising the key to its definition. "Die Aufgabe des Übersetzers" dislocates definitions rather than establishing them because, itself an uncanny translation of sorts, its concern is not the reader's comprehension nor is its essence communication.

> Is a translation intended for the readers who do not understand the original?. . . . What does a piece of writing "say"? What does it communicate? Very little to him who understands it. The essential is not communication, not assertion. . . . If [the translation] were aimed at the reader, the original would have to be also. If the original does not exist for him, how could the translation be understood in this respect?

> *Gilt eine Übersetzung den Lesern, die das Original nicht verstehen?. . . . Was 'sagt' denn eine Dichtung? Was teilt sie mit? Sehr wenig dem, der sie versteht. Ihr Wesentliches ist nicht Mitteilung, nicht Aussage. . . . Wäre [die Übersetzung] aber für den Leser bestimmt, so müßte es auch das Original sein. Besteht das Original nicht um dessentwillen, wie ließe sich dann die Übersetzung aus dieser Beziehung verstehen?* (IV.1.9)

If, one by one, once familiar words become incomprehensibly foreign, if they relentlessly turn on their past (*althergebrachte, herkömmliche*) meanings, if the essay systematically roots itself in that tradition only to shift the very ground it stands on, this, after all, is the way in which translation functions. For Benjamin, translation does not transform an original foreign language into one we may call our own, but rather, renders radically foreign that language we believe to be ours. Benjamin cites Rudolf Pannwitz:

> "Our translations, even the best ones, proceed from a false grounding: they wish to germanize Hindi, Greek, and English instead of hindicizing, grecizing, and anglicizing German. They have a much more significant respect for their own linguistic usage than for the spirit of the foreign work. . . . the fundamental

error of the translator is that he holds fast to the incidental state of his own language instead of letting it be violently moved by the foreign."

"unsre übertragungen auch die besten gehn von einem falschen grundsatz aus sie wollen das indische griechische englische verdeutschen anstatt das deutsche zu verindischen vergriechischen verenglischen. sie haben eine viel bedeutendere ehrfurcht vor den eigenen sprachgebräuchen als vor dem geiste des fremden werks . . . der gründsäztliche irrtum des übertragenden ist dass er den zufälligen stand der eignen sprache festhält anstatt sie durch die fremde sprache gewaltig bewegen zu lassen." (IV.1.20)

This invasion of the foreign is perhaps merely prescriptive for other translations, for the initial attack on his audience immediately gives way to a more amicable rhetoric of life, kinship, harmony, fidelity, religion, and nature. As in Baudelaire, where the wounds inflicted by "To the Reader" are soon to be soothed by the balm of "Correspondances," so in Benjamin's essay, it would seem we find ourselves again on native soil.[3]

In the metaphorical climate that now sets in, translations seem to promise the organic temporality of plant life: they blossom forth from the original as a continuation of that former "life"[4]—as a "transplant," a "ripening," a germination of the original "seed." But for all this apparently abundant flourishing, at no point does translation relate organically to the text that precedes it. On this point Benjamin is as ironical as he is deceptive. The *Entfaltung* ("unfolding" [IV.1.11]) that the life of the original achieves in translation never quite brings its seeds to flower.[5] Translation denies the linear law of nature in order to practice the rule of textuality. If the original cannot reach the realm of linguistic fulfillment "root and branch" (*mit Stumpf und Stiel* [IV.1.15]), this figure of speech, a metaphor for completion in both German and English, must also be taken in its "fully unmetaphorical reality" (IV.1.11). Nowhere in the essay does translation develop into the future promised by the germ (*keimhaft* [IV.1.12]), the kernel (*Kern* [IV.1.15]), the seed (*Samen* [IV.1.17]).

More precisely, this essential kernel is definable as that in translation which, in its turn is untranslatable. . . . Unlike the poetic word of the original, it is not translatable because the relation-

ship of content to language is completely different in the original
and the translation. If language and content constitute a certain
unity in the original, like fruit and rind, the language of translation envelops its contents in vast folds like an emperor's robes.
For this language signifies a loftier language than its own and
therefore remains non-adequate, violent and foreign with respect to its own content.

*Genauer läßt sich dieser wesenhafte Kern als dasjenige bestimmen,
was an ihr selbst nicht wiederum übersetzbar ist. . . . Es ist nicht
übertragbar wie das Dichterwort des Originals, weil das Verhältnis
des Gehalts zur Sprache völlig verschieden ist in Original und Übersetzung. Bilden nämlich diese im ersten eine gewisse Einheit wie
Frucht und Schale, so umgibt die Sprache der Übersetzung ihren
Gehalt wie ein Königsmantel in weiten Falten. Denn sie bedeutet
eine höhere Sprache als sie ist und bleibt dadurch ihrem eigenen
Gehalt gegenüber unangemessen, gewaltig und fremd.* (IV.1.15)

The natural metaphors for translation produce the opposite of organic
fruition. The *Nachreife* (literally, "after-ripeness" [IV.1.12 and 13]) hardly
completes the maturing process of the original, but rather, withers the
fruit of meaning. The "unfolding" of the original paradoxically results
in a proliferation of abundant folds that violently camouflage the content while maintaining it as non-adequate otherness. No further germination is possible: "This brokenness prevents any [further] translation, and at the same time makes it superfluous" (IV.1.15).

The *Verpflanzung* ("transplant" [IV.1.15]) of the original bespeaks far
less the continued life of the plant than a displacement of its ground:

This task of ripening the seed of pure language in translation
seems never to be solvable, to be definable in no solution. For is
not the ground pulled out from under such a language if the res-
titution of meaning ceases to be decisive? And indeed nothing
else—to turn the phrase negatively—is the significance of all the
foregoing.

*Ja, diese Aufgabe: in der Übersetzung den Samen reiner Sprache
zur Reife zu bringen, scheint niemals lösbar, in keiner Lösung be-*

stimmbar. Denn wird einer solchen nicht der Boden entzogen,
wenn die Wiedergabe des Sinnes aufhört, maßgebend zu sein?
Und nichts anderes ist ja—negativ gewendet—die Meinung alles
Vorstehenden. (IV.1.17)

With this negative turn of the phrase, Benjamin defines translation as undefinable. The unfixable task of translation is to purify the original of meaning: only poor translations seek to restore it (IV.1.9). This is why translations are themselves untranslatable. "Translations on the other hand show themselves to be untranslatable—not because of the heaviness, but because of the all too fleeting manner in which meaning attaches to them" ("Übersetzungen dagegen erweisen sich unübersetzbar nicht wegen der Schwere, sondern wegen der allzu großen Flüchtigkeit, mit welcher der Sinn an ihnen haftet" [IV.1.20]).

The relation between translation and original, then, although "seemingly tangible," is always on the verge of eluding understanding (IV.1.11). And eluding of understanding (*Erkenntnis*) is precisely what translation performs (*darstellt*). Benjamin insists on the verb *darstellen*, as opposed to *herstellen* or *offenbaren* (IV.1.12), for translation neither presents nor reveals a contents.[6] It touches on the meaning of the original only by way of marking its independence, its freedom—literally—to go off on a tangent: the point it chooses remains irrelevant.

What meaning remains of significance in the relation between translation and original can be grasped in a simile. Just as a tangent touches the circle fleetingly and only at one point, and just as it is the touching and not the particular point that dictates the law according to which it takes off on its straight trajectory further into infinity, so translation touches the original fleetingly and only at an infinitely small point of meaning in order to . . . follow its own trajectory.

Was hiernach für das Verhältnis von Übersetzung und Original
an Bedeutung dem Sinn verbleibt, läßt sich in einem Vergleich
fassen. Wie die Tangente den Kreis flüchtig und nur in einem
Punkte berührt und wie ihr wohl diese Berührung, nicht aber der
Punkt, das Gesetz vorschreibt, nach dem sie weiter ins Unendliche
ihre gerade Bahn zieht, so berührt die Übersetzung flüchtig und

> *nur in dem unendlich kleinen Punkte des Sinnes das Original,*
> *um . . . ihre eigenste Bahn zu verfolgen.* (IV.1.19–20)

Certainly, it is its own trajectory that "The Task of the Translator" follows when touching on such terms as "fidelity," "literality," and "kinship." These it translates from a familiar German to another that hardly seems germane. But that, after all, is the point. Nowhere is this unfamiliarity more intensely sensed than when the essay turns to the familial relations between languages. The "kinship" Benjamin sets out to describe gathers much of its strangeness from the discrepancy between his mode of defining and his ultimate intention of definition. If we are made at all familiar with the notion of kinship, it is by learning what kinship is not. Kinship between languages is not similarity (IV.1.12–13), nor can it guarantee the preservation, in translation, of the original's form and sense. Benjamin touches fleetingly here on a point of epistemological concern.

In order to grasp the genuine relation between original and translation, we must set up a deliberation whose design is completely analogous to the train of thought in which a critique of cognition demonstrates the impossibility of a mimetic theory. If there it is shown that no objectivity in knowledge could exist— not even a claim to it—if it consisted in duplication of the real, then it can be proven here that no translation would be possible if it strove with its total being for similarity with the original.

Um das echte Verhältnis zwischen Original und Übersetzung zu erfassen, ist eine Erwägung anzustellen, deren Absicht durchaus den Gedankengängen analog ist, in denen die Erkenntniskritik die Unmöglichkeit einer Abbildtheorie zu erweisen hat. Wird dort gezeigt, daß es in der Erkenntnis keine Objektivität und sogar nicht einmal den Anspruch darauf geben könnte, wenn sie in Abbildern des Wirklichen bestünde, so ist hier erweisbar, daß keine Übersetzung möglich wäre, wenn sie Ähnlichkeit mit dem Original ihrem letzten Wesen nach anstreben würde. (IV.1.12)

This explains why kinship may only be defined negatively. The kinship between languages generates their *difference:* on what basis could translation claim to duplicate the original if no language, however original, in turn guarantees the objective reality of that which it names? For all this insistence on kinship as differentiation, kinship sets forth a certain sameness as well. The elusive nature of this sameness presents particular difficulties to the English translator. In the long passage that speaks of this sameness, Harry Zohn remains far less "true" to the original, far less "literal" than the text demands.[7] This is because he maintains a significant respect for his own linguistic usage, and traditionally, that is to his credit. Understandably then, his translation results in phrases such as "the same thing," "the same object," where the German speaks neither of objects nor things. In an admittedly germanized English, the passage would read as follows:

> All suprahistorical kinship of languages rests in the fact that in every one of them as a whole . . . one and the same is meant [*gemeint*], which, however, is not reachable by any one of them, but only by the totality of their mutually supplementing intentions— pure language. While, namely, all individual elements of foreign languages—the words, sentences, contexts—exclude one another, these languages supplement one another in their intentions. To grasp this law, one of the fundamental laws of the philosophy of language, is to differentiate what is meant [*das Gemeinte*] from the manner of meaning [*die Art des Meinens*] in the intention. In "Brot" and "pain" what is meant is indeed the same; the manner of meaning it, on the other hand, is not. . . . While in this way the manner of meaning in these two words is in conflict, it supplements itself in both languages from which they are derived. The manner of meaning in them supplements itself into what is meant. In the individual, unsupplemented languages, what is meant is never found in relative independence, as in individual words or sentences; rather, it is grasped in a constant state of change until it is able to step forward from the harmony of all those manners of meaning as pure language.

> *Alle überhistorische Verwandtschaft der Sprachen [beruht] darin, daß in ihrer jeder als ganzer . . . eines und zwar dasselbe gemeint ist, das dennoch keiner einzelnen von ihnen, sondern nur der Allheit ihrer einander ergänzenden Intentionen erreichbar ist; die reine*

> *Sprache. Während nämlich alle einzelnen Elemente, die Wörter,*
> *Sätze, Zusammenhänge von fremden Sprachen sich ausschließen,*
> *ergänzen diese Sprachen sich in ihren Intentionen selbst. Dieses*
> *Gesetz, eines der grundlegenden der Sprachphilosophie, genau zu*
> *fassen, ist in der Intention vom Gemeinten die Art des Meinens zu*
> *unterscheiden. In "Brot" und "pain" ist das Gemeinte zwar das-*
> *selbe, die Art, es zu meinen, dagegen nicht. . . . Während dergestalt*
> *die Art des Meinens in diesen beiden Wörtern einander widerstrebt,*
> *ergänzt sie sich in den beiden Sprachen, denen sie entstammen.*
> *Und zwar ergänzt sich in ihnen die Art des Meinens zum Ge-*
> *meinten. Bei den einzelnen, den unergänzten Sprachen nämlich ist*
> *ihr Gemeintes niemals in relativer Selbständigkeit anzutreffen, wie*
> *bei den einzelnen Wörtern oder Sätzen, sondern vielmehr in stetem*
> *Wandel begriffen, bis es aus der Harmonie all jener Arten des*
> *Meinens als die reine Sprache herauszutreten vermag.* (IV.1.13–14)

What is meant by "Brot" and "pain" is "the same," but this is not to
say that they mean the same *thing*. The same that is meant is "pure
language." Benjamin states this quite literally at the beginning and end
of the passage, but a hunger for substance could well allow us to forget
it. What is meant by "pure language"? Certainly not the materialization
of truth in the form of a supreme language. Benjamin sets this temptation aside with a passage from the "Crise de vers" (IV.1.17). He displaces
his own text with the foreignness of Mallarmé's, in which the latter
insists on the insurmountable disparity between languages. The "pure
language" of the lengthy citation above does not signify the apotheosis
of an ultimate language (even at the end of history) but signifies rather
that which is purely language—nothing but language. "What is meant"
is never something to be found independently of language nor even
independently in language, in a single word or phrase, but arises instead
from the mutual differentiation of the various manners of meaning.
There is not quite so much difference as one might suspect, then, between "kinship" as sameness and "kinship" defined as differentiation,
for each generates the other, in language, indefinitely.

In a sense, one could argue, the kinship of language as here defined
says nothing after all. If so, the translation of Benjamin has been rendered with the great fidelity the essay requires. For the translator's task

of "fidelity" (*Treue*) calls for an emancipation from all sense of communication (IV.1.19), a regaining of pure language. The "one and the same" which is meant in pure language means nothing.

To win back pure language formed in the flux of language is the violent and single power of translation. In this pure language, which no longer means anything and no longer expresses anything—which, as expressionless and productive word, is that which is meant in all languages—all communication, all meaning, and all intention ultimately meet with a stratum in which they are destined to extinction.

Die reine Sprache gestaltet der Sprachbewegung zurückzugewinnen, ist das gewaltige und einzige Vermögen der Übersetzung. In dieser reinen Sprache, die nichts mehr meint und nichts mehr ausdrückt, sondern als ausdruckloses und schöpferisches Wort das in allen Sprachen Gemeinte ist, trifft endlich alle Mitteilung, aller Sinn und alle Intention auf eine Schicht, in der sie zu erlöschen bestimmt sind. (IV.1.19)

This productive word that renders meaning extinct is that of literality (*Wörtlichkeit*). In the text of translation, the word replaces sentence and proposition as the fundamental element (IV.1.18). Instead of conventional, natural reproduction, what results is a teratogenesis in which the limbs of the progeny are dismembered, all syntax dismantled.

Literality thoroughly overthrows all reproduction of meaning with regard to the syntax and threatens directly to lead to incomprehensibility. In the eyes of the nineteenth century, Hölderlin's translations of Sophocles were monstrous examples of such literality. . . . The demand for literality is no offspring of an interest in maintaining meaning.

Gar die Wörlichkeit hinsichtlich der Syntax wirft jede Sinneswiedergabe vollends über den Haufen und droht geradenwegs ins Unverständliche zu führen. Dem neunzehnten Jahrhundert standen Hölderlins Sophokles-Übersetzungen als monströse

Beispiele solcher Wörtlichkeit vor Augen. . . . Die Forderung der Wörtlichkeit [ist] unableitbar aus dem Interesse der Erhaltung des Sinnes. (iv.1.17–18)

The demand is Benjamin's, for it is this monstrosity that he praises above all as the most perfect of all translations. Hölderlin's translations are touched upon at three other points in the essay and always spoken of as exemplary.[8]

This exaction of literality, the passage continues, must not be understood as an interest in meaning, but "aus triftigeren Zusammenhängen" (iv.1.18). Must it be understood, then, "in a more meaningful context," as Zohn's first translation insists?[9] Or is the contextuality of original and translation such that this phrase too must be taken literally? The linking together of the two would then be *triftig* in its etymological sense—from *treffen*—as striking, fragmentary. This is certainly the point, if not the tone of the simile, that follows:

> Just as fragments of a vessel, in order to be articulated together, must follow one another in the smallest detail but need not resemble one another, so, instead of making itself similar to the meaning of the original, the translation must rather, lovingly and in detail, in its own language, form itself according to the manner of meaning [*Art des Meinens*] of the original, to make both recognizable as the broken part of a greater language, just as fragments are the broken part of a vessel.

> *Wie nämlich Scherben eines Gefäßes, um sich zusammenfügen zu lassen, in den kleinsten Einzelheiten einander zu folgen, doch nicht so zu gleichen haben, so muß, anstatt dem Sinn des Originals sich ähnlich zu machen, die Übersetzung liebend vielmehr und bis ins Einzelne hinein dessen Art des Meinens in der eigenen Sprache sich anbilden, um so beide wie Scherben als Bruchstück eines Gefäßes, als Bruchstück einer größeren Sprache erkennbar zu machen.* (iv.1.18)

In the literal translation above, the passage leaves things incomplete.[10] With the joining together of translation and original, language remains a broken part (*Bruchstück*). Such is the mode of Benjamin's articulation despite its apparent reference to organic growth, kinship, sameness, and fidelity. (And it is both the mode of articulation of baroque allegory, with its insistence on the ruin ["Allegory and Trauerspiel," in *Origin of German Tragic Drama*], and also the vision of the "angel of history" ["On the Concept of History," part IX].)[11]

Perhaps this helps account for the involuted formulation—translation must awaken from its own language the original's echo. This is not to say that translation, in coming after, echoes the original. Translation relates to the original as to pure language—in a way that the original, so laden with its apparent content, is rarely deemed to function.

In this lies a characteristic of translation totally different from that of poetic works, since the intention of the latter is never towards language as such, its totality, but rather solely and directly towards definitive linguistic coherences of content. Translation, however, does not view itself as poetry does—as in the inner forest of language—but rather as outside it, opposite it; and, without entering, it calls into the original, into that single place where, in each case, the echo is able to give in its own language the resonance of a work in a foreign tongue.

Hierin liegt ein vom Dichtwerk durchaus unterscheidender Zug der Übersetzung, weil dessen Intention niemals auf die Sprache als solche, ihre Totalität, geht, sondern allein unmittelbar auf bestimmte sprachliche Gehaltszusammenhänge. Die Übersetzung aber sieht sich nicht wie die Dichtung gleichsam im innern Bergwald der Sprache selbst, sondern ausserhalb desselben, ihm gegenüber und ohne ihn zu betreten ruft sie das Original hinein, an demjenigen einzigen Orte hinein, wo jeweils das Echo in der eigenen den Widerhall eines Werkes der fremden Sprache zu geben vermag. (IV.1.16)

To locate the source of these reverberations is not an easy matter. Though, logically, the original should originate the call, Benjamin's formulation leaves this task to translation.

There is an unmistakable echo here of a German saying that both amplifies and clarifies the predicament: "Wie man in den Wald hineinruft, so schallt's heraus" ("As one calls into the forest, so it will resound"). The proverb speaks of an unproblematic reverberation not necessarily at play in Benjamin's version of it. Still, translation's call into the forest of language is not a repetition of the original but the awakening of an echo of itself. This signifies its disregard for coherence of content, for the sound that returns is its own tongue become foreign. Just as the vase of translation built unlike fragment on unlike fragment, only to achieve a final fragmentation, so the echo of translation elicits only fragments of language, distorted into a disquieting foreignness.

But who pieces the vase together? Who sounds the echo? Which is to say, who writes the text of translation? Or are these questions that necessarily lose their meaning in the context of the essay? By now it is evident that when Benjamin speaks of "translation," he does not mean translation, for it has never ceased to acquire other, foreign meanings. One is tempted to read "translation" as a metaphor for criticism, to offer the answer that the critic writes translations. How else do we explain the following:

> Translation therefore transplants the original into a more—
> insofar as ironically—conclusive language realm, since it cannot
> be displaced from it through further translation. . . . The word
> "ironically" does not recall thoughts of the romantics in vain.
> They above others possessed insight into the life of works of
> which translation is the highest testimony. To be sure, they did
> not recognize translation as such, but turned their entire atten-
> tion to criticism.

> *Übersetzung verpflanzt also das Original in einen wenigstens inso-*
> *fern—ironisch—endgültigeren Sprachbereich, als es aus diesem*
> *durch keinerlei Übertragung mehr zu versetzen ist. . . . Nicht um-*
> *sonst mag hier das Wort 'ironisch' an Gedankengänge der Roman-*
> *tiker erinnern. Diese haben vor andern Einsicht in das Leben der*
> *Werke besessen, von welchem die Übersetzung eine höchste*
> *Bezeugung ist. Freilich haben sie diese als solche kaum erkannt,*
> *vielmehr ihre ganze Aufmerksamkeit der Kritik zugewendet.*
> (IV.1.15)

Translation may indeed be a metaphor for criticism,[12] but the critical text is inexorably bound to a certain irony. That irony dislocates the syntax of Benjamin's phrase above as well as the tentative solution to the question "who writes," in which our own critical distance was not ironical enough.

"Translatability"—which we might also call the critical text within—is a potential of the work itself: "Translatability belongs to certain works essentially—which is not to say that their translation is essential to them, but rather that a certain significance dwelling within the originals expresses itself in their translatability" ("Übersetzbarkeit eignet gewissen Werken wesentlich—das heißt nicht, ihre Übersetzung ist wesentlich für sie selbst, sondern will besagen, daß eine bestimmte Bedeutung, die den Originalen innewohnt, sich in ihrer Übersetzbarkeit aüßere" [IV.1.10]). This, then, is the text-ness of the text or a criticism without critic. From the very beginning, the essay dismisses the necessity of a translator for translation.

> Certain relational concepts maintain their good, perhaps best, sense . . . when they are not a priori exclusively referred to man. In this way one might speak of an unforgettable life or moment even if all men had forgotten it. That is to say, if its essence demands not to be forgotten, then that predicate would not correspond to something false, but rather, to a demand that does not correspond to man and would at the same time include a reference to a realm to which it does correspond—to a remembrance of God.

> *Gewisse Relationsbegriffe [behalten] ihren guten, ja vielleicht besten Sinn . . ., wenn sie nicht von vorne herein ausschließlich auf den Menschen bezogen werden. So dürfte von einem unvergeßlichen Leben oder Augenblick gesprochen werden, auch wenn alle Menschen sie vergessen hätten. Wenn nämlich deren Wesen es forderte, nicht vergessen zu werden, so würde jenes Prädikat nichts Falsches, sondern nur eine Forderung, der Menschen nicht entsprechen, und zugleich auch wohl den Verweis auf einen Bereich enthalten, in dem ihr entsprochen wäre: auf ein Gedenken Gottes.* (IV.1.10)

The translatability of the text excludes the realm of man and, with him, the translator, the figure to which Benjamin's essay is devoted. The

Aufgabe of the translator is less his task than his surrender: he is *aufge-geben*, "given up," "abandoned." This is the essay's initial irony.

Yet no sooner is the figure of man abandoned than another appears to offer itself. At the beginning and the end Benjamin turns to the realm of the theological, which seems to redeem this monstrous loss (if also, in a sense, to cause it). This is the way, in the essay's closing paragraph, he writes of Hölderlin's translations—the most perfect of their kind. The overwhelming danger they create may only be contained by the Holy Writ:

> Because of this there lives in [Hölderlin's translations] above all the monstrous and originary danger of all translation—that the gates of a language so expanded and controlled may fall shut and enclose the translator in silence. The Sophocles translations were Hölderlin's last work. In them meaning plunges from abyss to abyss until it threatens to lose itself in the bottomless depths of language. But there is a halt. However, no text guarantees it but the holy text.

> *Eben darum wohnt in ihnen vor andern die ungeheure und ürsprungliche Gefahr aller Übersetzung: daß die Tore einer so er- weiterten und durchwalteten Sprache zufallen und den Übersetzer ins Schweigen schließen. Die Sophokles-Übersetzungen waren Hölderlins letztes Werk. In ihnen stürzt der Sinn von Abgrund zu Abgrund, bis er droht in bodenlosen Sprachtiefen sich zu verlieren. Aber es gibt ein Halten. Es gewährt es jedoch kein Text außer dem heiligen.* (IV.1.21)

What is it exactly that the Holy Scriptures vouchsafe? Is it really a halt to the precipitous loss of meaning, or must we translate Halten rather as a holding and retaining of that loss. For in the Holy Scriptures meaning no longer separates language and revelation. The holy text is totally literal, in Benjamin's sense of the word, which is to say, because no meaning stands behind its language, because language and revelation coincide absolutely, it is as absolutely meaningless as an original may be.

> However, no text guarantees it but the holy text, in which mean- ing has ceased to be a watershed for the flow of language and the

flow of revelation. Where a text belongs to a truth or doctrine immediately, without the mediation of meaning, in its literalness of true language—that text is absolutely translatable. . . . Such boundless trust with respect to it is demanded from the translation that just as in this [holy text] language and revelation are united without tension, so in the translation, literality and freedom must join in the form of the interlinear version. For to some degree, all great writings—but above all, the Holy Scriptures—contain their virtual translation between the lines.

Es gewährt es jedoch kein Text außer dem heiligen, in dem der Sinn aufgehört hat, die Wasserscheide für die strömende Sprache und die strömende Offenbarung zu sein. Wo der Text unmittelbar, ohne vermittelnden Sinn, in seiner Wörtlichkeit der wahren Sprache, der Wahrheit oder der Lehre angehört, ist er übersetzbar schlechthin. . . . Ihm gegenüber ist so grenzenloses Vertrauen von der Übersetzung gefordert, daß spannungslos wie in jenem Sprache und Offenbarung so in dieser Wörtlichkeit und Freiheit in Gestalt der Interlinearversion sich vereinigen müssen. Denn in irgendeinem Grade enthalten alle großen Schriften, im höchsten aber die heiligen, zwischen den Zeilen ihre virtuelle Übersetzung. (IV.1.21)

And what of Benjamin's "between the lines," for from the beginning, we recognized this essay as a translation of sorts. Between the lines of German, he has slipped in a phrase from the original of the Holy Writ. It apparently speaks of the beginning of linear time and coincidently, therefore, posits both the origins of language and the condition of temporality which makes a conventional concept of translation possible.

Ἐν ἀρχῇ ἦν ὁ λόγος (IV.1.18). These are the opening words of the Gospel According to John, and the text to which Benjamin's clearly refers when it speaks of the Holy Scriptures. "Die Aufgabe des Übersetzers" serves as a translation for the following lines which are given below in an interlinear literal translation from Luther's version of the text.

1. Im Anfang war das Wort, und das Wort war bei Gott
1. In the beginning was the word, and the word was with God
      und Gott war das Wort.
      and God was the word.

2. Dasselbige war im Anfang bei Gott.

2. The same [the word] was in the beginning with God.

3. Alle Dinge sind durch dasselbige gemacht und ohne

3. All things are through the same made and without
   dasselbige ist nichts gemacht, was gemacht ist.
   the same is nothing made which made is.

This is the final irony.

Six

Emergency, Break

Things Will Never Be the Same (Again)

It is not that the past casts its light on the present or the present its light
on the past: rather image is that in which the Then [*das Gewesene*]
comes together with the Now [*Jetzt*] into a constellation like a flash of
lightning. In other words: image is dialectics at a standstill. For whereas
the relation of the present to the past is a purely temporal, continuous
one, that of the Then with the Now is dialectical: it is not process but
rather image, disconnected spring (*sprunghaft*). —Only dialectic images
are true (i.e. not archaic) images; and the place one happens upon them
is language.

—Benjamin, "N [Re the Theory of Knowledge,
Theory of Progress]" (N, 49)

Show and Tell

In a sense it is again a question of translation, although certainly not
directly. Perhaps no text of Benjamin fails to pose that question and to
perform it. "The Task of the Translator" is exemplary in this regard,
rendering incomprehensibly foreign each of its terms, offering us metaphors of seeds that germinate, flower, and ripen only to uproot them.
The same could be said of the essay that is our current concern, "Doctrine of the Similar"—particularly of the apparently critical term in that
title.[1] The etymological roots of *ähnlich* ("similar")—which we might
call a history of the word, or even a literal translation—are particularly
telling, even though different dictionaries insist on radically different
origins. The Duden points to a jumbling of two different words: the one
speaks of similarity, the other of unity. The Wahrig traces *ähnlich* to

Ahnen, den Ahnen gleich ("ancestors," "similar to ancestors"), and more precisely, to an Indo-Germanic *Lallwort* ("babble word") for ancestors. The woman is babbling, you are thinking. She supposes she can translate *ähnlich* by retracing its history to likeness, unity, ancestors, and similar nonsense, imagining this might give us insight into the realm of the "similar." But I never promised you insight—not in any simple sense—although Benjamin does, or seems to. "Insight into the realms of the 'similar,'" he begins his essay, "is of fundamental significance for the illumination of larger areas of occult knowledge" (11.1.204; DS, 65).[2] Let us forget for the moment that this is illumination of that which will necessarily remain obscure: by definition, insight into a realm that will remain occult, that is concealed. Still, I never offered you insight, but rather a history, and history is not quite the same as insight. I did this in solidarity with, or rather, in mimicry of Benjamin, who offers several histories of his own. Mimicry, after all, is the first example of the similar that Benjamin offers us in "Doctrine of the Similar," and it has a privileged position in the opening line of "On the Mimetic Faculty": "Nature engenders similarities," he writes. "One need only think of mimicry" (11.1.210; MF, 333). If natural mimicry, then, is an imitation of one's surroundings in order to conceal oneself,[3] my own mimicry performs the characteristic unity we never cease to expect from the reader with respect to text.

Benjamin's mimicry is his turn to history. Why history? Why repeatedly, as we shall see, an insistence on the temporalization of the question of similarity? How is this to be related to the suggestion that "insight into the realms of the 'similar' is . . . to be won less by showing similarities already hit upon than through the reproduction of the processes that engender such similarities" (11.1.204; DS, 65)? How does Benjamin's essay, his writing and our reading, not so much point to that which is similar as set the scene for a production of similarities? How might Benjamin's turn to the past bring about such engendering? For Benjamin is about to tell us two stories, the first a tale of childhood, the second a tale of ancestors: "This capacity, however, has a history, more particularly in the phylogenetic as well as the ontogenetic sense. With respect to the latter, play is its school in many ways. To begin with, children's games are everywhere interlaced with mimetic modes of behavior and their realm is in no way limited to what one human being imitates from another" (11.1.204–5; DS, 65).

In the ontogenetic history—that is, in the development of the individual—imitation is not limited to the human figure but reaches also to its other—which is not to say that nature is the object. What the child also imitates is the man-made: "The child plays not only [at being] merchant or teacher but also windmill or train." (II.1.205; DS, 65). Teacher and merchant, windmill and railroad: if the first two play a role in Benjamin's personal history,[4] the latter also have their histories. The windmill's history is literary, above all. Its revolutionary motion is an obvious foil to the linear progressive displacement in space of the train.

Benjamin had something to say about this in a commentary on one of Marx's metaphors: "Marx says revolutions are the locomotives of world history. But perhaps it's entirely different. Perhaps revolutions are the grasp of the human race traveling in this train for the emergency brake" (1.3.1232).[5] The passage is from notes peripheral to the theses "On the Concept of History." There as here, the thrust of historical progress is undercut by a revolution of another order.

At this point, Benjamin asks the ironical question of the use of mimetic behavior. The answer, he tells us, presupposes another history, a meditation on its phylogenetic significance:[6] "But the question it comes to is now this: precisely what kind of use/purpose this schooling in mimetic behavior brings?" (II.1.205; DS, 65). Where are we going with this mimicry, and what will it profit us? (These, of course, questions engineer and merchant would not fail to ask.) To answer this we must look to a larger historical frame than that of the individual—namely, to the broader "experience of similarity . . . in the course of history" (II.1.205; DS, 65). For the answer to the question of use "presupposes clear meditation [*Besinnung*] about the phylogenetic meaning of mimetic behavior" (II.1.205; DS, 65)—a return to our ancestors, so to speak.

Whatever other turns this history may take, its first chapter is governed by a rhetoric of mensuration. Size and number are the parameters of significance, with terms such as "tiny," "small," "much larger," "micro-" and "macro-," "countless many," and "innumerable" (II.1.205). Yet, these terms of measure are indeed incalculable, making no pretensions to concrete or absolute quantification (just as later in the essay the word makes no claim to concrete or absolute designation). They operate only in the mode of comparison.

First, our present is contrasted to a past in which the law of similarity played over a much vaster realm. "As we know, the sphere of life that once seemed to be ruled by the law of similarity was much larger. It was the microcosm and macrocosm, to name only one version of many that the experience of similarity thus found in the course of history" (ii.1.205; DS, 65). But then, in a shift both abrupt and scarcely readable, we find the two eras, that were at first counterposed, now sharing common ground: in both, conscious perception of similarities is far less usual than their unconscious determination: "Still now, for those living today it can be maintained: the cases in which they daily *consciously* perceive similarities are a tiny segment of those innumerable cases in which similarity determines them *unconsciously*" (ii.1.205; DS, 65, emphasis added).

How can we gain insight into this shift in ground? And might it or its failure threaten with an abyss into which all theory threatens to fall? Benjamin begins here by setting up the distinction between two time periods, one ancient and one our own. Why does the difference between eras vanish in the wake of another difference, that between consciousness and unconsciousness? Why is the distinction between consciousness and unconsciousness such that unconsciousness (and even nonperception) becomes all but overwhelming? What is the significance, if any, of a passage that begins by talking of similarities as they seem to take place in the sphere of life—in other words, that begins by talking *about* similarities—but then turns to engendering them, even though that turn may be all but imperceptible? Does this have something to do with Benjamin's pronouncement "The gift we possess of seeing similarity is nothing but a weak rudiment of the formerly powerful compulsion to become similar and behave in a similar manner" (ii.1.210; DS, 69)? Moreover, why does production of similarities take place as simile and in the name and form of unconsciousness? "Those similarities that are perceived *consciously*—for example, in faces—are compared [*verglichen*] to those countless similarities, perceived *unconsciously* or not at all, like the enormous underwater block of the iceberg in *comparison with* the small tip that one sees rising out of the water" (ii.1.205; DS, 65, emphasis added).

Is this the "clear meditation on the phylogenetic significance of mimetic behavior" that will enable us to answer "what kind of use/purpose schooling in mimetic behavior brings"?[7] For as the passage compares conscious perception and countless unconscious perceptions to the form of an iceberg, it suddenly moves more like a windmill than like a locomotive. If "*a* is to *b* as *c* is to *d*" usually lays the ground for traditional proportion, the equality of two ratios (perhaps also the assurance that all is well with the alphabet), here *a* is to *b* as *d* is to *c*.[8] What turns that ratio on its head? Why, just when Benjamin produces similarities, does comparison fail to progress as it should? This, in a flash that disrupts the order of conscious perception.

Still, something is of use in this comparison even though it goes off in the wrong direction. In the name of all these correspondences, once again there is concern with a certain response: "These natural correspondences, however, get their decisive significance only in light of the consideration that they are all fundamentally stimulants and arousers [*Erwecker*] of that mimetic faculty which gives them a response [*Antwort*] in humans" (II.1.205; DS, 65). If the answer in the opening line of Benjamin's previous paragraph ("The response presupposes the clear meditation on the phylogenetic significance") was to the question of profit ("what kind of use/profit this schooling in mimetic behavior brings"), here, "response" is hardly so pointed. The "natural correspondences" seem to awaken the mimetic faculty in us which thus offers them an answer of sorts. It is this that gives to those correspondences their "decisive significance." But of which "natural correspondences" does Benjamin speak? Is it those of the *natural* simile of the iceberg, the dangers of which one tends to see only the tip? Is it the natural correspondences "in faces," the example Benjamin gives of consciously perceived similarities ("those similarities that are perceived *consciously*— for example, in faces"), for these have an equally unsettling history in Benjamin's writings.[9] Or is it the correspondences—so much more difficult to see at first glance—the correspondences structured so seductively in the natural mimicry of the language, which can equally be read as stimuli (*Stimulantien*) or response?

Certainly, the natural response to this disrupted sequence of nonevents would be to return to the historical, genetic (or degenerate) thrust with which the essay begins. This is the all-too-understandable response that such awakenings of the similar arouse.

> Thereby one must consider that neither the mimetic forces nor the mimetic objects, their objects, remain unchangeably the same *in the course of time*; that *in the course of the centuries* the mimetic force, and along with it *later,* also [*gleichfalls*] the mi-

metic faculty of perception, has disappeared out of certain fields, perhaps in order to pour forth in others. Perhaps the assumption is not too bold that *a uniform direction in the historical development* of this mimetic capability is recognizable. (II.1.205; DS, 65–66, emphasis added)

Here the unidirectional course of the centuries accounts for the differentiation in mimetic forces, mimetic objects, and also (later) the mimetic faculty of apprehension. Or is this a mistaken perception? Is perception, perhaps, bound to be a mistake? Isn't what one beholds—for example, "the small tip that one sees rising out of the water" (II.1.205; DS, 65)—more a warning about what one does not see than an object one can take at face value? "*On first glance* the direction could lie only in the increasing decline [*Hinfälligkeit*] of this mimetic faculty" (II.1.205–6; DS, 66, emphasis added). Yet it is less that the mimetic faculty has simply died, Benjamin tells us, than that it has been transformed, less that it has disappeared altogether than that it "has disappeared out of certain fields perhaps in order to pour forth in others" (II.1.205; DS, 66). The problem is one of following the direction in which this transformation has taken place. It will not be simple, certainly not direct. It is the concern of the critical passage that follows, in which astrology will be our model. In which direction such a transformation of the mimetic faculty may lie "something can be gathered from astrology, even if indirectly" (II.1.206; DS, 66).

To be sure, astrology will ultimately serve as a point of comparison, although it will be presented as a matter of history. What we can take away from it (if we do not wish to go away entirely empty-handed) what we can gather from it, if only indirectly, is the direction taken by the transformation of the mimetic faculty, the ostensible difference between the two eras. This means, from the beginning, taking into account a certain loss. As those who research what has been handed down by the ancestors, we must take into account a loss which we are not capable of suspecting, much less apprehending. That of which we can have no premonition, no presentiment, is the "sinnfällige Gestaltung" (II.1.206)—literally, the formation that might fall to the senses, as a "mimetic character of the object" (II.1.206; DS, 66).

"For example, in the constellations of the stars" (II.1.206; DS, 66). For example, perhaps, but hardly a neutral example in Benjamin's writings.

Show Time

Let us get our bearings before we go further, recapitulate where we are and how we have come here. The issue is that of the similar, of course. That goes without saying. The method, however overcome by detours it has been, is history—or rather histories, the ontogenetic and the phylogenetic. To be sure, as we turned to the comparison between us and our ancestors, we did get off track—possibly losing the answer to the question of profit and purpose to a response [*Antwort*] appearing as the production of similarities. And this took place precisely in the moment when Benjamin's language spoke in simile (the simile of the iceberg). But whatever turn that might have given to the line of argument, we have returned here to thinking that is structured along the lines of "course of time," "course of the centuries," "course of history," the era "of the modern human being" in contrast to the "ancient peoples" or "primitives" (II.1.205–6; DS, 65–66).

Still, we have been warned that it is perhaps less a matter of extinction of the mimetic faculty than of transformation, that it is perhaps less a question of disappearance than of a pouring forth where we least expect it, and that if we are to gather anything about the direction of change over the course of time, it will be only indirectly. This will call for a new mode of reading indirectly, which is to say that one cannot plan for it in advance, cannot map out a strategy that will then be carried through. To read: what was never written.

How are we to grasp the constellation, for example—"For example, in the constellations of the stars." (II.1.206; DS, 66)—given that those objects to be imitated, that fall to the senses, were there where we are incapable of suspecting them? The response Benjamin produces to this apparent loss is above all in terms of a temporal ordering of before and after. This temporalization takes place not only in the course of history but also in the names both of interpretation and of a repeated insistence on the mimetic as *Nachahmbarkeit*—an imitation that comes after.

History, interpretation, and imitation—all these are on the line here. The story Benjamin tells of history: Once upon a time, among those who lived earlier, certain objects fell to the senses, yet now they do not. The story of reading: Once there was a horoscope and then there was an astrological interpretation that followed; the constellation first presents a unity and only then does an interpretive cognition take place: "In order to grasp that, the horoscope must be comprehended above all, at one time [*vor allem einmal*] as an *originary* totality which is only analyzed in the astrological interpretation. (The star cluster [*Gestirnstand*] displays [*darstellt*] a characteristic unity and [it is] *first* in their operation in the star cluster that the characters of the individual planets are recognized.)" (ii.1.206; DS, 66, emphasis added). The story of imitation: First there were events, that which preceded as model and example, and then these were imitated. "One must, fundamentally, take into account that events [*Vorgänge*] in heaven were imitable by those who lived earlier" (ii.1.206; DS, 66). The imitability of a similarity already present (*vorhanden*) seems to indicate the possibility of dealing with it: "Indeed . . . this imitability [*Nachahmbarkeit*] contained the instruction to deal with a similarity already present to hand" (ii.1.206; DS, 66). But in this essay that plays continually on the hand, what can be grasped cannot necessarily be held fast, and the possibility of leaving empty-handed has everything to do with the question of the similar. "For the time being [*bis auf weiteres*] one must regard this imitability by humans . . . as the sole basis on which astrology has been given its experiential character" (ii.1.206; DS, 66, emphasis added). How else, then, might we regard the experiential character of astrology (Benjamin's example that was to illustrate our incapacity of suspecting the presence of the mimetic object) if not with respect to imitability by humans? For such a take on the matter, we have just read, is only provisional [*bis auf weiteres*].

The time being of which he speaks apparently has no duration. It flits past. For Benjamin immediately changes direction with a characteristic "but" that abruptly resituates our perspective: "But if, really, mimetic genius was a life-determining force of the ancients, then it is hardly possible not to attribute complete possession of this gift to the newborn, especially the perfect formation according to [*Anbildung*] the cosmic form of being" (ii.1.206; DS, 66). Suddenly it is a question of the newborn in a pronouncement that will rewrite the temporal expectations of "similarity." It might seem for an instant yet to be a question of imitability, *Nachahmbarkeit*, a conventional sense of human beings born under a certain configuration of the stars. But *Anbildung* ("imaging on," "imaging according to") is not *Nachbilden* ("imaging after"). If, above, the mimetic genius is "a life-determining force of the ancients," the opening lines of the essay relate a similar story with respect to humans in general. It is humans who "possess the very highest capability of producing similarities," and there are no human "higher functions which are not decisively co-determined by the mimetic faculty" (II.1.204; DS, 65).

However, this is not to say that humans imitate a natural or cosmic scene outside them. Benjamin makes this as clear as he can when the temporality of his "for the time being" is replaced by the instant (*Nu*). The question of birth—which is to say, the determining moment of humans in their relation to the mimetic faculty (perhaps the determining moment of the human, period)—cannot be viewed in the course of time (except theatrically): as the once-upon-a-time of history in its relation to a present, as a story of decay or for that matter of progress, as a text of imitation of that which preceded it, or of an interpretation added to that which is present to hand. "The moment of birth [*Augenblick*, literally, 'glance or flash of the eye'] that should be decisive here is, however, but an instant [*Nu*]" (II.1.206; DS, 66). With this second *aber* ("but") Benjamin changes direction again; in that moment, the eye is turned elsewhere: "This detours our glance [*Blick*] to another peculiarity in the realm of similarity. Its perception is in every case bound to an instantaneous flash [*Aufblitzen*]" (II.1.206; DS, 66). The moment of birth and the moment of perceiving similarity are, it would seem, similar, if not identical. That is to say, it is as though human life were determined, or, at least, the perceiver born, in that strange flash of perception.

This moment that turns the glance off course (and places the eye in question) calls for another conception of reading. With respect to the perception of similarity,

> its perception is in every case bound to an instantaneous flash. It flits by, can perhaps be won back, but cannot be held fast like other perceptions. It offers itself to the eye just as fleetingly, transitorily as a constellation of stars. The perception of similarities thus appears bound to a moment of time. It is like the supervention [*Dazukommen*] of the third, of the astrologer, to the conjunction of two stars that wishes to be grasped in the moment [*Augenblick*]. (II.1.206–7; DS, 66)

The temporality of sequence that determined almost all that preceded—the histories told of similarities and the temporality of the perception of similarities that seems analogous to that of history, mimesis, and interpretation—is consumed in a flash. As Benjamin offers the example of the constellation, bound both to birth and to the actual reading of the stars, the scenario of historian or reader appearing belatedly to imitate or interpret what was already present to hand is abruptly abandoned. Perception here is no longer a question of possession: it "cannot be held fast like other perceptions" (II.1.206; DS, 66). Perception of similarities implies a rewriting of our understanding of such terms as *erfassen* ("grasp") and *besitzen* ("possess") (II.1.206 and 207).[10] In the instantaneous flash of similarity the astrologer does not see the constellation or name it from the outside. Unlike the astronomer, the astrologer appears with no tools of observation and can expect no reward. "In another instance the astronomer, despite the sharpness of his tools for observation, is cheated out of his reward" (II.1.207; DS, 66). Rather, in this newly conceived moment of interpretation the reader-astrologer—this is what is so astonishing—both completes and is assimilated into the constellation in a flash,[11] a constellation that is not one until the astrologer joins the two stars that otherwise form no figure at all.

And yet, we have not quite gotten it. For we have all but forgotten (and how could it be otherwise) that Benjamin speaks in similes once again. If he apparently speaks of this perception as that which cannot be held fast, he performs that evasion in the gesture of comparison.[12] The perception of similarities offers itself to the eye *as* fleetingly *as* a constellation, in a moment that is *like* the formation of a constellation, a constellation that at once, unimaginably, inscribes and is read by the astrologer.

With the figure of the constellation, we seem to enter familiar territory, however ironically such recognition must be viewed. For could we not claim that in the Proust essay which preceded "Doctrine of the Similar" and in the theses "On the Concept of History" which followed it, something very similar takes place?[13] Benjamin, of course, refuses to proclaim aloud the most important thing he has to say. Thus, he poses, like an insect, amid an intricate foliage structured to look like linear time, until a spring, a beat of wings, a leap or sentence, shows the startled observer that an incalculable rupture has taken place here. The true reader of Benjamin is constantly jarred by such shocks.

In the Proust essay Benjamin places his reader in search of past time, just as in "Doctrine of the Similar" it is the multiple histories that set the trajectory of the opening pages. In mimicry of Proust, who sets the trap of the past only to spring it, Benjamin produces a biographical chatter about Proust's life [*Leben*] to do almost the same. In the one as in the other, the reach towards that which has already happened collapses the temporal distance between periods in the flash of a moment which at once dispels any sense of mimetic recuperation of either past or self. Not surprisingly, it is in a world of similarities that all this takes place, and here, a certain image or constellation is bound to suddenly appear.

> That is Proust's frenetic study, his impassioned cult of similarity.... The similarity of one thing to another that we count on, that occupies us while awake, merely plays around the deeper similarity of the dreamworld in which what takes place never emerges as identical, but rather as similar, opaquely similar to itself.... Torn by homesickness, he lay on his bed, homesickness for the world distorted in the state of similarity.... To it belongs what takes place in Proust—and how carefully and elegantly it arises. Namely, never isolatedly lofty and visionary, but rather heralded and multiply supported, bearing a fragile, precious reality—the image. (ii.1.313–14; ip, 204–5)

If in the constellation of "Doctrine of the Similar" it is just when the observer grasps (at) what she sees that she becomes a part of its configuration, in "Towards the Image of Proust" Benjamin gives us several formulations to mark this lapse. Benjamin compares Proust's reach towards his past self to a game children play with a rolled up stocking from the laundry basket: with a grasp towards those contents he empties the dummy that seems to be a past self and transforms it into the image (ii.1.314; ip, 204–5). Or he will speak, for example, of "the work of the *mémoire involontaire,* of the rejuvenating force" as "a match for relentless aging." "When the past [*das Gewesene*] mirrors itself in the dew-fresh 'instant', a painful shock of rejuvenation snatches it up once again . . . as incessantly as . . ." (ii.1.320; ip, 211). But rejuvenation and consumption, bringing to mind and loss, are therein indistinguishable. "Proust performed the monstrous act of letting the entire world *age* by an entire human life in an instant. But precisely this concentration, in which what otherwise simply wilts and dims consumes itself in a flash, is called rejuvenation [*Verjüngung*]" (ii.1.320; ip, 211).

How could this fail to remind us of that other essay, demystifier of recuperative temporality and locus of other instantaneous flashes, Benjamin's last work, the theses "On the Concept of History"? That essay sets forth a relentless critique of the concept of time as linear, empty, and homogenous. Restoring the past "as it really was" (1.2.695; TH, 255) operates in complicity with a concept of progress: and both are the province of historicism, which Benjamin distinguishes over and over again from what he chooses to call "historical materialism." As in "Doctrine of the Similar," where the progressive structure of decline is suddenly challenged by the constellation and a concept of language which we will see disrupts the apparently linear and causal relationship between word and signified; as in "Towards the Image of Proust," where memory is inexorably interwoven with forgetting, where "rejuvenation" brings about "aging" in the flash of a moment—so in the "On the Concept of History": constellation, shock, monad, standstill, the countermovements to the progressive and recuperative models of historicism.[14] If historicism implies a fall from the past that can be remedied in the teleological " 'eternal' image of the past" (1.2.702; TH, 262) in which "the truth will not run away from us" (1.2.695; TH, 255), if the concepts of "period of decline" (v.1.575; N, 48) and progress go hand in hand, both in the way in which the course of time is conceived and also in the saving act of historicism, Benjamin's messianic Nowtime (*Jetztzeit*) is quite different. Time stops and comes to a standstill (1.2.702; TH, 262).

> To thinking belongs not only the movement of thoughts but also their bringing to a standstill [*Stillstellung*]. Where thinking suddenly stops in a constellation [*Konstellation*] sated with tensions, there it imparts to the constellation a shock by which it crystallizes itself as a monad. The historical materialist approaches a historical object there and only there where he encounters it as monad. In this structure he recognizes the sign of a messianic arrest [*Stillstellung*] of happening. (1.2.702–3; TH, 262–63)[15]

> Historicism provides the 'eternal' image of the past, the historical materialist an experience [*Erfahrung*] with it which alone stands forth. (1.2.702; TH, 262)

> It is an irretrievable image of the past that with each present threatens to disappear. (1.2.695; TH, 255)

With the flitting by of the simile of constellation, nothing will ever be the same again: not for the historical materialist in the encounter with the past, not for Proust as the writer of a memoir, not for the astrologer of "Doctrine of the Similar." For in the latter the mimetic faculty of perception (which earlier in the essay was bound to a mimetic object that fell to the senses [II.1.206; DS, 66]) has disappeared from one field in order to pour forth in another, that of "non-sensuous similarities" (*unsinnliche Ähnlichkeiten*). The indirection to which the moment of birth of the human, as reader/writer of the constellation, has led is that of non-sensuous similarity. And while the remaining pages of the essay will touch once again on history and imitation, while they also make a singular hint at sense, they will do so always with a flash of irony.

Nowhere is this irony more dazzling than when Benjamin insists that "that which is signified" (*das Bedeutete*) is that which gives rather than receives the name. "Thus the letter Beth has the name of a house" (II.1.208; DS, 67). *Beth* in Hebrew is the second letter of the alphabet and is also the noun used to mean "house." Yet Benjamin insists here that "house" is the name-giver. Letter, name, thing (that which is signified [*Bedeutete*] or meant [*Gemeinte*]), as well as spoken and written word enter into a relationship in which all sense of fixed and predictable priority and hierarchy (say, of the anteriority of the signified with respect to the name) seems to vanish with all sense.[16]

The disordering of the terms of the iceberg simile is a similar performance, breaking the linear continuum and prioritization associated with the logic of comparison. So is Benjamin's disruption of the concept of onomatopoeia. He may speak of how "imitating behavior was granted its place in the origin of language as an onomatopoeic element," but "such considerations [remain] most closely bound to the common (sensual) realm of similarity" (II.1.207; DS, 67). Despite the conventional understanding of onomatopoeia as the sensual imitation that follows the natural sound of the represented object, Benjamin's sense of onomatopoeia is neither sensual nor *Nach*ahmung (an imitation that follows). Thus, when he asks, "Can a sense be said to underlie the proposition [*Satze*] which Leonhard maintains in his instructive work 'The Word': 'Every word is—and the entire language is—onomatopoeic'?"[17] the answer is yes only provisionally. "The key which actually first makes this thesis fully transparent lies concealed in the concept of a non-sensuous similarity" (II.1.207; DS, 67). The entire language is onomatopoeic with respect to itself in the literal sense of the term, as a making of the name. In such moments as the flashing [*Aufblitzen*] up of the constellation, language is capable of making itself, each instant anew, in a fully new, originary, underivable way.

We no longer possess "in our perception . . . what once made it possible to speak of a similarity that exists between a star constellation and a human" (II.1.207; DS, 66). From what we have just read, it seems we never did. What we might be said to possess, if possession could still have meaning here, does not so much make non-sensuous similarity understandable as bring its unclarity in greater proximity to clarity—elucidating, then, that which nevertheless cannot be definitively grasped. "There would be . . . a polarity of the centers of the mimetic faculty in humans. It shifts from the eye to the lip" (II.3.958). What we possess, Benjamin tells us, is the canon of language (II.1.207; DS, 67).

Performance, Time

"Doctrine of the Similar" pretends to tell of a fall from a privileged state of language and to tell it in the guise of histories. Isn't this a story we have already heard, read at least, more or less, once upon a time? Not quite the same story, from a certain perspective perhaps the inverse, and yet there are similarities. "On Language as Such and on the Language of Man," written almost at the beginning of Benjamin's opus (1916) speaks of the language of man (perhaps both in and about it). Mimicry of another text, it too tells or retells a story—a history of origins that it borrows from Genesis. Like those stories of "Doctrine of the Similar," it is set against the most ancient of days and will mark the origins of human language.

Even before it brings us back to the Garden of Eden, "On Language as Such" speaks of the relation between "the mental essence of a thing" and "its language" (II.1.141; OLaS, 315) This was the implicit question of "Doctrine of the Similar" that culminated in the constellation, and it is the essay's explicit concern once Benjamin turns to "non-sensuous similarities." Above all, then, there is this similar question, floating at the outset of the 1916 essay, which will later point to an originary naming, the naming that God performs, and after him Adam.

And if Benjamin is less than decisive on the relationship between these two—between "the mental essence that communicates itself" and "language itself"—this is because here, almost from the beginning, it is not a matter of show and tell but of performance and time.

> It is therefore first of all self-evident that the mental essence that communicates itself in language is not language itself but rather something to be distinguished from it. The view that the mental essence of a thing consists precisely in its language—this view understood as a hypothesis is the great abyss into which all theory of language threatens to fall, and to maintain itself just floating over the abyss is its task. (II.1.141; OLaS, 315)

How are we to understand this? (For later Benjamin will frame such issues precisely in terms of knowledge.) Certainly not as a definitive insistence that the "mental essence" that communicates itself in language is not language itself. What we are given to understand for the moment, "for the time being" so to speak, is that understanding this identity *as a hypothesis* ("this view, understood as a hypothesis") is an abyss that threatens all theory of language. And if one here lets one's eye fall to the note at the bottom of the page, Benjamin underscores that the threat of the abyss lies in its relation to hypothesis, which is to say, in the positioning of this insistence on identity at the outset: "Or is it rather the temptation of placing the hypothesis at the outset that creates the abyss for all philosophizing?" (II.1.141n; OLaS, 315n).

If we must not take this identity of the mental essence of the thing and its language as a hypothesis, such a formulation, apparently, nevertheless will paradoxically have its place.

> The differentiation [*Unterscheidung*] between a mental essence and a linguistic essence in which it communicates is the most originary in an examination of language theory, and this difference seems to be so unquestionable that it is rather that the often maintained identity between mental and linguistic essence forms a deep and ungraspable paradox whose expression was found in the ambiguity of the word Λόγος. Nevertheless, as solution this paradox has its place at the center of linguistic theory; it remains, however, paradox and insoluble if it stands at the beginning. (II.1.141–42; OLaS, 315)

This paradox does indeed find its place, if not at the beginning then at the "center" of Benjamin's essay on linguistic theory. For the following pages repeatedly make this assertion of identity.

The paradox has something to do with an abyss into which all theory of language and all philosophizing threatens to fall. This is the fall that Benjamin later will speak of as "a knowledge [*Erkenntnis*] from outside, the uncreative imitation of the creating word" in which the name steps outside itself (II.1.153; OLaS, 327), in which, paradoxically (considering the warning against hypothesizing the identity of thing and language), thing and language are to be distinguished. "The Fall is the moment of birth of the *human word* [in which] the word should communicate *something* (other than itself). That is really the Fall of language-mind" (II.1.153; OLaS, 327). What the opening pages of "On Language as Such" perform in their refusal to assert the identity of language and thing *as hypothesis*—that is, as knowledge from the outside—is to float above the abyss. And isn't the abyss paradoxical precisely because whether one falls into it or floats over it must remain up in the air. For once one proclaims the identity between thing and language as knowledge, the assertion separates them in its act of cognition. The "Fall of language-mind" is there at the moment of its fullest affirmation. We float here the implausibility of fall as a definitive event in Benjamin's theory of language, and it will come up again later.

This temptation of a fall in a text that will soon speak of Genesis, of beginnings, of knowledge, of language, and above all of *the* Fall cannot be taken lightly. "On Language as Such" seems to carry us, above all, back to an era before what "Doctrine of the Similar" calls "decline," before what theology calls the Fall. If Benjamin interrupts his own story, splits its grounds, constituting its movement in the break of deferral, the story he retells from the Bible is one of a language in which, it would seem, there is a seamless continuity between mental being, thing (*Ding*), and language (*Sprache*).

At least in God. God creates nature (Genesis 1) in the "rhythmics" of "Let there be—He made (created)—He named" (II.1.148; OLaS, 322). In the "Let there be" at the beginning and the "He named" at the end of the act, "the deep, clear relation of the act of creation to language appears every time" (II.1.148; OLaS, 322–23). Language is that which creates as Word and that which completes as name. "In God the name is creative, because it is word, and God's word is cognizant [*erkennend*] because it is name" (11.1.148; oLaS, 323). Only in God, however, is there such an absolute relationship to cognition, and only in God is the name identical to the creating word. Man's naming is not quite the same: "God made things knowable [*erkennbar*] in their names. Man, however, names them according to knowledge [*Erkenntnis*] (11.1.148; oLaS, 323).

How are we then to speak of Adamic naming in which, it would seem, the relation between thing and language is not quite what it is for God. "Man is the knower of the language in which God is the creator. God created him in his image; he created the knower in the image of the creator" (11.1.149; oLaS, 323). If it is only in God that the absolute relation of name to knowledge takes place, how are we to think the difference of cognition in Adamic naming? For human language or naming, unlike that of God, is not creative. "Name fails to reach Word just as knowledge [fails to reach] creation" (11.1.149; oLaS, 323). Human language is not creative word but, rather, name as reflection of the Word (*Reflex des Wortes*).

Benjamin's language has its own word to mark the difference of human cognition in Adamic naming. It is "conception" (*Empfängnis*) (11.1.150; oLaS, 325) (a word that Benjamin could have cited from language theories of the previous century).[18] Some version of the word appears five times in the course of nine lines, like densely sown seeds promising a certain germination. It marks the difference between God's naming of things and man's as it marks the point of articulation of name and thing: "In [human] naming the word of God has not remained creative; it has become on one part conceiving, even if conceiving [*empfangend*] language. This conception is directed to the language of the things itself, from which in turn, soundlessly, in the mute magic of nature the Word of God shines forth" (11.1.150; LS, 325).

To figure the relationship between God and humans in an act of conception is hardly original. It is to this derivative concept that we will have to return even though Benjamin is all but silent on the matter. Rather than speak of it directly, he substitutes another term that will prove equally seminal in its excessive repetition—"translation."

> But for conception and spontaneity together—how they are
> found only in the linguistic realm in this uniqueness of union—
> language has its own word. . . . It is *translation* of the language of
> things into those of humans. It is necessary to ground the con-

> cept of translation in the deepest level of language theory. . . . It
> gains its full meaning [*Bedeutung*] in the insight that every
> higher language (with the exception of the Word of God) can be
> regarded as the translation of all the others. Translation is the
> leading over of one language into the other through a con-
> tinuum of transformations. Translation passes through con-
> tinuums of transformation, not abstract areas of identity and
> similarity. (II.1.150–51; OLaS, 325, emphasis added)

Thus, language has its own word for conception: "translation" (*Übersetzung*). Translation is the leading over from one language into another
and above all from the language of things into the language of man.[19]
However paradisiac Adam's naming may be, translation from the language of things into that of humans brings about human knowledge;
and the knowledge of man, Benjamin never ceases to remind us (and
how could we forget it in the Garden of Eden?), is not the same as that
of God. "Translation cannot avoid adding something, namely knowledge" (II.1.151; OLaS, 325). "This knowledge of the thing [*Sache*] is, however, not spontaneous creation" (II.1.150; OLaS, 324).

  Already in naming, then, already in translation, there is a foretaste of
the fruit of the tree of knowledge and of the Fall. For whereas Benjamin
will insist on the difference between the perfect knowledge (II.1.152;
OLaS, 326) of Adam in paradise and the knowledge of good and evil,
whereas he will distinguish Adam's naming from the (fallen) human
word that communicates something (*etwas mitteilt*), is there not, nevertheless, a strange double register to "translation" that places it both
before and after the Fall?

> As the mute word in the existence of things lags so endlessly far
> beneath the naming word in the knowledge of man, as this, in
> turn, [lags] beneath the creative Word of God, thus is the ground
> given for the multiplicity of human languages. The language of
> things can pass into *the* language of knowledge and naming only
> in translation—so many translations, so many languages namely
> once man has fallen out of the paradisiacal state that knew only
> one language. (According to the Bible, of course, this result of
> the expulsion from paradise only came later.) (II.1.152; OLaS, 326)

According to the Bible, but what about according to Benjamin? For in the passage above, translation within Eden leads over almost immediately into translation outside it—through a continuum of transformations. It is not a question here of equating Benjamin's concept of Adamic naming to naming after the Fall. But given the story of the tower of Babel, "translation" is, after all, a remarkably tainted term for the relation between thing and human language in Paradise.

It goes without saying that the word which "translation" replaces in the course of Benjamin's discourse is no less maculate: "conception" (*Empfängnis*). How can one read of the relation between God and human as conception without reading what was never written there: the adjective "immaculate," although in this particular essay of Benjamin it is manifestly absent?[20] This method of reading is one Benjamin might have called "performance as detour" (1.1.208; OGTD, 28).[21]

Translation, then, in all its duplicity offered in place of a conception bound to and blasted by spontaneity—conception, which, in turn, we might be tempted into saying, comes to us marked with a certain history. For the immaculate conception is the doctrine that claims that the Virgin Mary "in the first instant of her conception . . . was preserved exempt from all stain of original sin," the only human born not subject to the original sin that resulted in the fall of Adam and Eve.[22] What does it mean, then, that in telling the story of Adam, Benjamin refers to the relationship between man and God with a term that inevitably echoes that other "conception," a conception destined to erase, so to speak, the sin of eating from the tree of knowledge?

The New Testament is claimed to read the Old as its typological repetition, a repetition said to promise revelation and redemption[23]—for the Virgin, let us not forget, is regarded as the Second Eve.[24] Redemption through repetition: how, then, should we read Benjamin's reading of Genesis by way of an echo of the New Testament in that critical term *conception,* which, according to Catholic doctrine, marked the unique exception to the consequences of the Fall? Conception in "On Language as Such" is, once again, the point of articulation between man and God, and Benjamin's term is not *im-maculate.* Moreover, his conception therefore necessarily floats not only the question of redemption in its relation to the Fall, but also the question of reading.

Following on the Old and New Testaments, Benjamin's text is the third in line in the lineage we seem to be tracing, if we do not get caught in the echoes of a term that is something of a temptress. For if language has a word for the connection and difference between God's name and Adam's, and if that word, "conception," cites the New Testament while also, as Benjamin insists, marking the intersection of God/Adam/language, there are, perhaps, other names besides "conception" for this border between the cognizing name of man and the creative word of God. They are names that Benjamin barely utters, and then only parenthetically. It is perhaps audacious, but hardly impossible, to call this border between man and God "woman-and-Eve."

Still, it is not I who said it originally, but rather, Benjamin and, before him, Adam.

> The deepest image [*Abbild*] of this divine Word and the point at which human language achieves the most intimate participation in the divine infinity of the pure Word . . . that is the human name. The theory of the proper name is the theory of the border between finite and infinite language. Of all beings man is the only one that names his own kind himself, as he is also the only one that God did not name. Perhaps it is daring but hardly impossible to name verse 2.20 in its second part in this context: that man named all beings "*but*" for man no helpmate was found who was fit for him. Accordingly, Adam names his wife as soon as he has received her. (Woman in the second chapter, Eve in the third.) (II.1.149; OLaS, 323–24)

Benjamin reads the *aber* ("but") of Genesis (just as we read the "but" of Benjamin) as a rupture and change in direction.[25] In the context of a theory of the proper name, he audaciously places Adam's double naming[26] at the border between the finite language of man and the infinite language of God, situates woman/Eve at the conjunction of human language and God's creative Word. For in Genesis Adam names his female counterpart twice, "woman" in the second chapter and "Eve" afterwards; names her once in her innocence, and names her again in original sin. From the beginning has the cliché not held true: have these not been the only names for the female of the species—virgin and temptress? Thus, the typological reading has the Virgin Mary appearing in the New Testament as the Second Eve—coming forth immaculately conceived and entirely free of the original sin into which Eve tempted Adam.

Let us say, however, with Benjamin: "In every epoch the attempt must be made anew to win tradition from a conformism that is about [*im Begriff steht*] to overpower it" (1.2.695; TH, 255). Following on Eve in the Old Testament and Mary in the New, how shall we then regard that third (and fourth) figure, that appears in "On Language as Such" in the guises of "woman" (*Männin*) and "Eve" (*Heva*), parenthetically. She appears at the site of conception, just where the proximity of God's naming to Adam's naming is at issue, which is more or less the site of translation. And, like translation, woman is doubly named almost in the same breath, once before the Fall and once after, in a proximity so close that one wonders wherein the difference between the two might lie. Implicitly rereading the immaculate reconception of Eve in the story of Mary, Benjamin goes against the grain of this history, conceiving the female differently, *doubly*, as woman-and-Eve. She is necessarily made maculate by a history that in its citation of Genesis enacts what Benjamin, in a gesture of radical translation of the New Testament's conception of the term, will later choose to call *redemption*. However, "it is not that Bible interpretation is pursued as goal, nor is the Bible at this point objectively taken as the basis for contemplation as revealed truth; rather, that which emerges of itself out of the Bible text with regard to the nature of language should be detected" (II.1.147; OLaS, 322).

What is performed here is a mode of writing and reading that ironizes the teleological structure of typological interpretation. It ironizes as well any misconception of Benjamin's Messianism. Benjamin's reading is not interpretation as goal or revealed truth. It breaks the genetic tale of God's creation followed by Adam's language, Eve's fall, and the redemption Mary promises; and it also breaks the progressive lineage of biblical texts—in the double name of woman/Eve. Neither the name of originary innocence nor the name of original sin, yet both at once, it preempts the logic of the originary, the Fall, and also of redemption as teleology. The third, doubly named woman/Eve involves a new mode of reading because she cannot be envisioned or named simply as innocence, or as Fall, or as redemption. "Woman/Eve" bursts forth in an unthinkable constellation of all these possibilities, and Benjamin situates her alongside Adam's participation through naming in the divine infinity of God's Word. She blasts the continuum of history, whether one wishes to see it as progression or as decay. "The overcoming of the concept of 'progress' and of the concept of a 'period of decline' are merely two sides of one and the same thing [*Sache*]" (v.1.575; N, 48). She also disrupts any conception of reading as bringing about either revealed truth or its loss.

In this moment of conception and translation, which is *the* moment of human language, the moment when it participates most intimately in the "divine infinity of the pure Word," where the "proper name" operates as the "communion of man with the *creative* word of God" (II.1.149–50; OLaS, 323–24), much is at stake. Not least of all is the concept of man ("Adam" in the Hebrew of Genesis operates not only as a proper noun for the first man but also as a common noun for mankind in general)[27]— the concept of man conceived in the image of God, his self-definition, how he names himself, how he utters his proper name or the closest thing to it, how he "himself names his own kind [*seinesgleichen*]" (II.1.149; OLaS, 324). For Adam calls his mate *woman*, an extension of himself. At the originary point that differentiates the genders (which, not coincidentally, is the critical point in the history of human language), the near-identity (the similarity) of the two (man/woman) is asserted. For Adam, his proper name and the name of his own, that most similar to him [*seinesgleichen*], almost come together. Adam uttering "woman" is like the naming of himself, yet is also the naming of the other, as female, in an act that is very similar to that of simile. Human language as naming and naming as simile. Here is "the reproduction of processes that . . . engender similarity" (II.1.204; DS, 65), again. Like Adam before him, Benjamin's naming of woman/Eve is like the addition of a third to the conjunction of two stars that wished to be grasped in the moment.

"On Language as Such" and "Doctrine of the Similar" give narrative histories of the loss of a paradisiacal state of language. Similar tales might equally be structured as teleologically redemptive. In Benjamin's work from beginning to end, ironically, this complicity and interchangeability of a banal concept of redemption with that of the Fall is at play. This is what takes place in "Towards the Image of Proust," for example, where Benjamin's reader might be lured into finding either a nostalgia for a lost past (in a temporality of fall) or a celebration of its recuperation as redemption. What takes place instead is the production of the dialectical image. In the theses "On the Concept of History" the messianic arrest of thought shatters both the sense of progress and that of decline. What I have attempted to articulate critically in each essay of this book, however, is the emergency brake of a moment, an abyss, a border. Call it, if you will, "constellation," "image," "redemption," "conception," "translation," "woman," and "Eve." These terms may be similar, but they are certainly not identical. It is not precisely that I claim to read these terms objectively or to reveal their truth. For is not reading for Benjamin "what never was written"? This is not only to say the obvious,[28] that reading, coming afterwards, produces something utterly different from its textual object. "What never *was* written, to read" (II.1.213; MF, 336). Reading is a writing but one that Benjamin ultimately refuses to put in any simple relation to "the past" (V.1.576; N, 49). If I were to find a simile for it I might say it is like the moment of the birth of the human, like the moment of Adam's self-naming both as woman and other, like the gesture of the historical materialist.[29]

So this is the story I have been trying to tell you, still uncertain whether it has progressed along as it should, uncertain whether it has either a clear or a happy ending, or even if it has any redeeming qualities. I have told it, necessarily, in the voice of woman, which, as you must recognize, is one way or another bound to Babel.

Notes

One: Letters from Walter Benjamin

1. "Truth," Benjamin writes, "is not unveiling which destroys the secret, but rather manifestation [*Offenbarung*] which is suitable to [the secret]" (1.1.211; OGTD, 31).

2. Much of what precedes is taken from *Trauerspiel* (1.1.207–10; OGTD, 28–30).

3. Benjamin will also speak in terms of the "treatise" (*Traktat*) (1.1.208; OGTD, 28).

4. Something similar takes place when Benjamin speaks of philosophical history: "That which is grasped in the idea of the origin still has history [*Geschichte*] only as a content [*Gehalt*], no longer as something that happens [*Geschehn*], by which it would be affected" (1.1.227; OGTD, 47).

Two: *Berlin Chronicle*

1. Walter Benjamin to Gerschom Scholem, February 28, 1933, in *The Correspondence of Walter Benjamin and Gershom Scholem: 1932–1940*, ed. Gershom Scholem (New York: Schocken, 1989), 27.

2. The discussion of the lost page and other editorial difficulties is in the afterword to the 1970 publication of *Berlin Chronicle*: Walter Benjamin, *Berliner Chronik* (Frankfurt am Main: Suhrkamp, 1970), 128–29.

3. *Steinschneider* means "gem cutter, lapidary, stone engraver." To be sure, Benjamin could not have known her name as one of his future editors, nor was she married to Steinschneider at the time. But, as irony would have it, that same letter of February 28, 1933, in which he announces the completion of the *Berlin Childhood* also mentions her name, as do many subsequent letters of his correspondence.

4. See Samuel Weber's fine reading of the term *Darstellung* in "Criticism Underway: Walter Benjamin's Romantic Concept of Criticism," in *Romantic Revolutions,* ed. Kenneth R. Johnston (Bloomington: Indiana University Press, 1990), 317.

5. Burckhardt Lindner uses the metaphor of the snapshot in "The *Passagen-Werk,* the *Berliner Kindheit,* and the Archaeology of the 'Recent Past,' " *New German Critique* 39 (Fall 1986): 26.

6. "Among the picture postcards in my album there were a few of which the written side has lasted better in my memory than their picture side" (VI.503–4; BC, 44). The passage that follows these lines from *Berlin Chronicle* has much affinity with the play on *Steglitz* that we will trace.

7. The *Berlin Chronicle* version, just quoted in translation, reads in German: "Der Irrgarten um Friedrich Wilhelm III und die Königin Luise die auf ihren bebilderten Empiresockeln mitten aus Blumenbeeten wie von den magischen Zügen versteinert strebten . . ." (VI.465). In this "Irrgarten," where the king and queen "strebten," how can one fail to read a rebus—those puzzles of which Benjamin was so fond and of which he wrote a few himself. It is a rebus of a line from Goethe, about whom Benjamin wrote and planned to write so much: "Es irrt der Mensch, solang er strebt" (Johann Wolfgang Goethe, *Goethes Faust* [Hamburg: Christian Wegner, 1903], 18). This, the solution to the puzzle, sets up another enigma, since the center of the labyrinth, the locus of the striving or struggle, is once again the place in which one goes astray.

8. See Rainer Nägele's commentary on the Medusa in his exceptional book, *Theater, Theory, Speculation: Walter Benjamin and the Scenes of Modernity* (Baltimore: Johns Hopkins University Press, 1991), 122–25. In another context, and from another perspective, Werner Hamacher speaks of writing in Benjamin as "a Medusa who petrifies the reader." Werner Hamacher, "The Word *Wolke*—If It Is One," in *Benjamin's Ground,* ed. Rainer Nägele (Detroit: Wayne State University Press, 1988), 157.

9. Henry Vizetelly, *Berlin under the New Empire* (London: Tinsley Brothers, 1870), 209.

10. Elsewhere, Benjamin uses the image of the blotting page as that which unwrites the written: "My thinking relates to theology like the blotting page to the ink. It has entirely sucked itself full with it [*Es ist ganz von ihr vollgesogen*]. If the blotting paper had its way, nothing that is written would remain" (1.3.1235).

11. As the opening lines of *Berlin Childhood around 1900* will insist (IV.1.237).

12. If in the succeeding lines this written space of his life turns out to be a map of Berlin, the coincidence would seem to go without saying. See VI.466–67; BC, 5.

13. Like that of which Scholem will write (Gershom Scholem, *Walter Benjamin—Die Geschichte einer Freundschaft* [Frankfurt am Main: Suhrkamp, 1975]; published in English as *Walter Benjamin: The Story of a Friendship*, trans. Harry Zohn [Philadelphia: Jewish Publication Society of America, 1981]).

14. "Outskirts" are a recurrent image in Benjamin's work. See, for example, his rebus on the term *Weichbild* (VII.1.302).

15. We might remember that it is also a question of genealogical trees in much of 1 Chronicles in the Old Testament—a text that does not fail to mention Benjamin (and Gershom), among many others.

16. The entire question of the tombstone in Goethe's *Die Wahlverwandtschaften* (pt. II, ch. 1) is relevant here.

17. See especially the closing lines of the fourth of the *Duino Elegies* (Rainer Maria Rilke, *Gesammelte Gedichte* [Frankfurt am Main: Insel, 1963], 455–56). Benjamin knew Rilke in his Munich years and had in any case been an admirer of his writing. See Benjamin to Carla Seligson, August 4, 1913, in Walter Benjamin, *Briefe* (Frankfurt am Main: Suhrkamp, 1966), 1:87.

18. The reference is probably to Epicurus's *Letter to Herodotus*. See A. A. Long and D. N. Sedley, *The Hellenistic Philosophers* (Cambridge: Cambridge University Press, 1987), 1:72–73. My thanks to John Peradotto for his help in locating the passage.

19. There is an important connection to be made here to Benjamin's insistence in his early essay "On Language as Such and On the Language of Man," on the non-instrumentality of language—on its operation as "medium" (II.1.142; OLaS, 315–16).

20. And, after all, "allegories are, in the realm of thoughts, what ruins are in the realm of things" (I.1.354; OGTD, 178). We might remember in this regard the connections Benjamin makes between criticism and Darstellung in *The Concept of Art Criticism in German Romanticism* (I.1.109). Or, to put it in a biographical perspective, we might remember the notice to *Illuminationen* that tells us that Benjamin's father was an antiquarian and art dealer and that there were archaeologists in the family (*Illuminationen* [Frankfurt: Suhrkamp, 1961], 439).

21.   See "Was Ist das Epische Theater?" II.2.534–35 and 537, for example.

22.   "Paris as it disclosed itself to me in the character of a hermetic tradition that I can follow back at least to Rilke . . . was more than a foliage-labyrinth [*Irrgarten*] a tunnel-labyrinth [*Irrstollen*]. Impossible to think away . . . the underworld of the metro and the North-South that opened itself up in the whole city with hundreds of shafts" (VI.469; BC, 9).

23.   The wood itself, as we know, is in turn metaphorical for Berlin and *Berlin*, for the forest of genealogical trees and blotter leaves.

24.   An excellent, as yet unpublished translation of *Berlin Childhood ca 1900* by Shierry Weber Nicholson (cited as BCh) is the source for some of the quotations here (often vastly modified to fit the precise terms of the argument).

25.   In Albert Heintze, *Die deutschen Familiennamen* (ed. Paul Cascorbi [Hildesheim: Georg Olms, 1967], 323), the name Lehmann is identified as "der kein eignes Erbe hat, sondern eines zu Lehen trägt, vasallus." Similarly, Wolfgang Fleischer, *Die deutschen Personennamen* (Berlin: Akademie Verlag, 1964): "*Lehmann* ist der *lehen-man*, der ein Grundstück von einem Grundherrn zu Lehen hat."

26.   Although, strangely enough, Steglitz Street was never oriented in the direction of its namesake, Steglitz.

27.   *Handwörterbuch des Deutschen Aberglaubens,* ed. E. Hoffmann-Krayer and Hanns Bächtold-Stäubli (Berlin: de Gruyter, 1936) 8:481, among other sources.

28.   Hamacher, "The Word *Wolke*," 152–54.

29.   Gerschom Scholem to Benjamin, August 1, 1931, in Scholem, *Walter Benjamin: The Story of a Friendship,* 169–74.

30.   With the wisdom of hindsight this would call on us to reread the scene in the Tiergarten and the involuted relationships among the water-script, the statues of the sovereigns, the carvings on the pedestal, the child who contemplates these, and Benjamin as he writes *Berlin Chronicle*.

Three: Walter Benjamin: Image of Proust

1.   Although the English translations are my own, for the reader's convenience I have provided page references to Harry Zohn's translation of this essay (in *Illuminations,* ed. Hannah Arendt (New York: Schocken, 1969), marked, as indicated in the list of abbreviations, with IP.

2.   The German word *Bild* may refer to a picture, a portrait, or a metaphor.

3. The earlier part of the passage indicates that similarity implies nonidentity: "the deeper similarity of the dreamworld in which what takes place *never emerges as identical but only as similar—impenetrably similar* to itself" (II.1.314; IP, 204, emphasis added).

4. Much more can be said about the relationship between Benjamin's passionate interest in surrealism and the issues of resemblance and noncoincidence in the writings of the surrealists. One should not, moreover, forget that Benjamin's essay "Surrealism" (II.1.295–310) was written at the same time as "Towards the Image of Proust." The interpenetration of the two essays is evident in Benjamin's insistence in "Surrealism," not only on the dream, but also on the image:

    > Life only seemed worth living where the threshold between waking and sleep was worn out in everyone as though from the steps of enormous numbers of images flooding back and forth, language [only seemed] itself where sound and image, image and sound, in that manner so successfully interpenetrated one another with automatic precision, that no crack was left for the penny "sense." Image and language take precedence. (II.1.296; S, 178–79)

    For a book-length study of Benjamin and surrealism, see Margaret Cohen, *Profane Illumination* (Berkeley and Los Angeles: University of California Press, 1993).

5. It is the original *Illuminationen* (ed. Siegfried Unseld [Frankfurt: Suhrkamp, 1961], 365) that has the emphatic *raumverschränkten*. In the *Gesammelte Schriften* the term used is *verschränkten*.

6. That remembrance, a temporal process, should play the role of time is hardly surprising: time functions here as a medium through which coincidence with past life is rendered possible. Why aging should play the role of space will become evident when, later in the passage, aging is seen to involve the forming of the image. A similar structure already appeared in the woven text description where remembrance and forgetting were counterposed. Remembrance, just as in the present passage, can be seen to figure as time. Since forgetting was called ornamentation and brought forth the spatial patterns of the woven carpet, it can be seen to figure as space.

7. Discussed on pp. 41–43 of this essay.

8. Benjamin writes of forgetting: "Every morning, awakened, we hold in our hands, mostly weakly and loosely, only by a couple of fringes, the tapestry of lived existence as forgetting wove it in us" (II.1.311, IP, 202).

9.   See the passage cited on p. 47 of this essay.

10. We should no longer find it strange that the physiognomy functions as metaphor for the Proustian image. This terminology was carefully heralded twice before in the essay, first in the definition of Proust's image ("The image [*Bild*] of Proust is the highest physiognomic expression . . ."), and later at the end of Part I of the essay: in Proust's world "the true surrealistic face of existence breaks through. To it belongs what takes place in Proust—and how carefully and elegantly it arises. That is, never in isolation, lofty and visionary, but rather heralded and multiply supported, bearing a fragile, precious reality—the image" (II.1.314; IP, 205). The physiognomy also plays a key role in "Myslowitz, Braunschweig, Marseille."

Indeed, *physiognomy* was a critical term throughout Benjamin's work. In "Das dämonische Berlin" Benjamin wrote:

> As you have heard, perhaps, one calls people physiognomists who look at and consider [*ansehen*] another person's face, or gait, or hands, or view [*ansehen*] his character in the form of the head, or his profession or even his fate. Thus, Hoffmann was less a perceiver [*Seher*] than a viewer [*Anseher*]. That is the valid German translation of *physiognomy*. And a major object of his viewing was Berlin, the city and the people who lived there. (VII.1.89)

Thus, *physiognomy* for Benjamin implies the broader act of reading and interpreting and is not limited to the contemplation of the human countenance.

See Rainer Nägele, *Theater, Theory, Speculation* (Baltimore: Johns Hopkins University Press, 1991), 47–48 and 72, who speaks of physiognomy in Benjamin as a counterforce to psychology and as an insistence on exteriority (104–7).

11. As one passes from memory of life to the image in the passages already read and a fourth yet to be discussed, a vocabulary of time bound up with interiority and depth—*Erinnerung* (II.1.311; IP, 202); *Restauration des Ursprünglichen* (II.1.313; IP, 204); *eingerollt, was drin liegt* (II.1.314; IP, 205); *Reflexion* (II.1.320; IP, 211); *Innerste, innersten Schwingen, tiefste Schicht* (II.1.323; IP, 214)—gives way to a vocabulary of space, surface, texture, and a rising to the surface—*Weben, Ornamente, verschlungener Arabesken* (II.1.311; IP, 202); *entleeren, auftauchen, zum Durchbruch kom-*

men (11.1.314; 1P, 205); *verschränkte, außen, Verschlingung, Vegegenwär-
tigung* (11.1.320; 1P, 211); *Runzeln und Falten, Eintragungen* (11.1.321; 1P,
211); *Bild* (11.1.314; 1P, 205); *Züge, Gesichtsbilder, Gebilde, Bilder, diesen
Fang zu heben* (11.1.323–24; 1P, 214).

The concept of time from which Benjamin distances himself is that
of the conventional interpretation of Proust's *mémoire involontaire:* time
as a medium for restoration through memory. The reader encounters
this naive interpretation of time: it offers a deceptive promise of coincidence and unity in which the present moment seems capable of mirroring and re-presenting the past. However, the ascendancy of the woven
carpet of forgetting, the passage to the dream world of nonidentity, and
the shock of aging introduce spatial difference (the *Bild*) and show the
coincidence of two points of time to be impossible. The particular roles
played by time and space are somewhat arbitrary, and it would be false
to conclude that the direction of movement in the passages—from time
to space—implies a simple priority of space over time. The space-
crossing of time indicates the movement in which discrepancy takes
place and out of which the image emerges: this discrepancy is concerned
rather with an intersection of the two than with a priority of either. And
although it is not the case in Benjamin's essay, one could imagine another movement through which discrepancy takes place, a movement
that proceeds from a naive concept of the spatial image into which temporal difference is introduced.

12.   "Homesickness for the world distorted in the state of similarity, in
which the true surrealistic face of existence breaks through. To [this
world] belongs what takes place in Proust . . . bearing a fragile, precious
reality—the image" (11.1.314; 1P, 205). "Not reflection [*Reflexion*]—
bringing to mind [*Vergegenwärtigung*] is Proust's method. [Proust] is
imbued with the truth that we all have no time to live the true dramas of
existence that are allotted to us. That makes us age. Nothing else. The
wrinkles and folds in our faces are the recordings [*Eintragungen*] of the
great passions, of the vices, the knowledge [*Erkenntnisse*] that called on
us" (11.1.320–21; 1P, 211–12).

13.   The "ornament" is the woven carpet of lived experience, yet demands
the forgetting of life: both the stocking and Proust's dummy seem to indicate a contents but turn out to be empty: the physiognomy is the record of past life, yet indicates our absence to that life.

14. It is here that we may see the preposition in Benjamin's title "Zum Bilde Prousts" as more significant than its apparent conventionality would suggest. The movement "towards" the image is never definitively completed.

15. Jacques Derrida's formulation is very similar to what takes place in Benjamin: "Without referring back to a 'nature,' the immotivation of the trace has always *become*. In fact, there is no unmotivated trace: the trace is indefinitely its own becoming-unmotivated" (*Of Grammatology* [Baltimore: Johns Hopkins University Press, 1974], p. 47).

16. The "new reality" that Benjamin speaks of here refers to his earlier description of the image as a "fragile, precious reality" (II.1.314; IP, 205), and the movement away from reflection on life that brings about the traits of aging obviously recalls the formation of the image-physiognomy in the opening pages of part III of the essay.

17. Although it is not within the scope of this essay, a more elaborate study of "Towards the Image of Proust" would take into account the complex play that Benjamin makes on specific passages of *A la recherche du temps perdu*. This particular description of Proust, for example, refers to the comparison between Michelangelo and Vinteuil in *La prisonnière* (Bruges: Bibliothèque de la Pléiade, 1954), 3:254–55.

18. "Torn by homesickness he lay on the bed. Homesickness for the world distorted in the state of similarity, in which the true surrealistic face of existence breaks through. To [this world] belongs what takes place in Proust . . . the image" (II.1.314; IP, 205).

19. See the discussion on pp. 53–54.

Four: Benjamin's Tessera

1. The story was first published in November 1930 in *Uhu*. The translations from this text are mine.

2. It is a preoccupation also of other works of Benjamin, such as "Die Unterschrift" ("The Signature") (IV.2.758–59). (For a sense of the broader implications and subtleties of this text, see Henry Sussman, *Franz Kafka, Geometrician of Metaphor* [Madison, Wis.: Coda Press, 1979], 14–17.) This is a story that—how can it be otherwise?—was also not quite his own. "Die Unterschrift"—which, significantly enough, is mentioned in the first protocol of Benjamin's drug experiences (VI, 558)—is found in a different version in Ernst Bloch's "Potemkins Unterschrift" (in *Spuren*, [Berlin and Frankfurt: Suhrkamp, 1959], 144–46, originally published in

1930), where Bloch writes that he in turn took it from Pushkin. One might reflect on the similarities between the names of the authors and their characters: *Pushk*in—Pet*ushk*ow, *Wal*ter Benjam*in*—Schu*walkin*; or that between Petushkow and Petukow, the characters of Pushkin and Bloch. Ernst Bloch, incidentally, or perhaps not so incidentally, appears as a character in "Myslowitz—Braunschweig—Marseille"—in fact, as the character more or less at the root of the story-telling.

3. In *Berlin Chronicle* Benjamin makes much of precisely the same transformation by an *i*—from "Steglitz" to "Stieglitz" (vi.472; *BC*, 12). See Chapter 2, above.

4. The metaphor is hardly as striking in German as in English, since in German *Gift* ("poison") is often used in relation to intoxication (e.g., *Rauschgift, rauschgiftsuchtig*).

5. Friedrich Nietzsche, *The Birth of Tragedy*, sects. 14 and 15.

6. That is, to the midnight ringing of church bells that closes the story and with it any possibility of Scherlinger's fortune, echoed in turn by the resonant clarity of the narrator.

7. See, for example, *Berlin Chronicle* (vi.486–87; *BC*, 25–26) and also the whole question in that text of reading the city like a labyrinth.

8. In *Trauerspiel* the mosaic is one of the images Benjamin proposes for philosophical contemplation:

    Just as the majesty remains for mosaics with their fragmentation into capricious little pieces, so philosophical contemplation is also not fearful of springing [*Schwung*]. . . . The value of thought fragments is all the more decisive the less they are able to directly measure themselves according to the fundamental conception, and the brightness of the presentation [*Darstellung*] is dependent on this [value] to the same extent that the value of the mosaic depends on the quality of the glass paste. (1.1.208; *OGTD*, 28–29).

9. In ways that we cannot note without interrupting the tactics of this argument, Benjamin's text is punctuated not only with the laughter and smiles that seem to break out almost anywhere, not only with the repeated promise of treasure we have begun to glimpse, but also with a constellation of terms that change their significance with the change of context. A few examples: *Zug* functions as facial feature (*Gesichtszug*, iv.2.735) but also refers to a mountain range (*Gebirgszug*), to the necessity of the move in chess (*Zugzwang*), and to a parade. The term *Fremde*

alternately means "tourist," "stranger," or "foreigner" (iv.2.731, 732, 736).
The key word *Stein* appears as chess piece (iv.2.730), quarries
(*Steinbrüche,* iv.2.731), the emblem of the holy stone (iv.2.737), and the
story's final word play, the stone bench (*Steinbank*). Also, of course,
Haar appears three times in ways discussed in the following text. The
manner of play on *Braun-schweiger* that is the open preoccupation of
Scherlinger's thought, then, is everywhere in the narrative.

    We might call these transformations or translations or even
onomatopoeia, as Benjamin's essays on language ("On Language as
Such" and "Doctrine of the Similar") variously would suggest.

10.   Following his "old travel rule" the painter avoids the "center of the
strange city—to explore first the outer districts." There, he bears witness
to the battle between city and country (iv.2.730–31). In the close combat
of telegraph poles (Tele*grafen*stangen) against agaves (*Agaven*), barbed
wire (*Stachel*draht) against thorny palms (*stachlige* Palmen) one senses
that it is the linguistic echoes that determine the state of struggle as
much as the apparent oppositions. If he follows the Rue de Lyon, it
culminates in an explosion that scatters the "splinters of [various] languages" along its route. The wanderings in Marseille are a linguistic ex-
ercise of sorts, then, but also an oscillation between figures of fullness
and emptiness that suggest something of what is to come.

11.   A *Scherling* is a shorn fleece. With reference to a similar passage in
Berlin Childhood, Werner Hamacher notes the juxtaposition of "a place
of sensuous enjoyment" with "a place where something is snipped":
"Doubts leveled me whether this box [with fine needles and shears in
various sizes] was exclusively for sewing—they were like those doubts
that now often came over me on an open street, when I cannot decide
whether I see a bakery or a barber shop" (quoted in Hamacher, "The
Word *Wolke*—If It Is One," in *Benjamin's Ground,* ed. Rainer Nägele
[Detroit: Wayne State University Press, 1988], 160).

12.   See "Hashish in Marseille" (iv.1.412; HiM, 140).

13.   With regard to the face folded in on itself, one might remember what
Benjamin writes in *Berlin Chronicle* of the Proustian "fan of memory"
(vi.467; BC, 6) where one finds ever new articulations in which no image
suffices, although it is only in the folds that *das Eigentliche* ("the real
thing") resides. Or one might think of Benjamin's description of the language of translation enveloping "its content like a king's robe in wide
folds" (iv.1.15). But perhaps most relevant of all are the lines in "Towards

the Image of Proust": "The wrinkles and folds in the face, they are the recordings of the great passions, of the vices, the knowledge that called on
us—yet we, the masters, were not at home" (II.1.321; IP, 211–12).

Renunciation functions in no simple way for Benjamin. He explicitly ironizes "the long-standing comfortable perspective" of the work of
art as "renunciation, heroism, asceticism" in "Towards the Image of
Proust" (II.1.313; IP, 204).

14. All this is worked through in greater detail in Chapter 6. One begins to
perceive here the similarities among a number of gestures: that of naming as both consumption and renunciation in "Myslowitz, Braunschweig, Marseille"; that of remembrance (as in "Towards the Image of
Proust," say, or *Berlin Chronicle*); that of perceiving similarities (in
"Doctrine of the Similar"); and that of the redemption promised in the
messianic power of historical materialism. In "On the Concept of History" the past, rejected as a sequence of causally connected events
(I.2.704; TH, 263), becomes cited in almost the same terms as the constellation read in "Doctrine of the Similar": "The true image of the past
flits past. Only as image that, never to be seen again, flashes up just in
the moment of its cognizability is the past to be seized" (I.2.695; TH,
255). The historian "grasps the constellation into which with a very determined earlier one his own epoch has entered" (I.2.704; TH, 263).

15. "On Language as Such," Benjamin tells us, is a reading of the opening
chapters of Genesis (II.1.147; OLaS, 321–22). Genesis 2:10–14 describes the
four heads of the river that went out of Eden. Each of these corresponds
to a (sometimes otherwise enigmatic) term at the close of Scherlinger's
tale, once again suggesting Scherlinger as a parodic version of Adam in
the Garden. The first branch "compasseth the whole land of Havilah,
where there is *gold*." The second "compasseth the whole land of *Ethi-
opia*." The third "goeth toward the east of *Assyria*," the nation of Sardanapalus. And the fourth, the river Euphrates (although its location is
not mentioned in Genesis) geographically joins the Tigris to form Satt
al-*Arab* (all emphases mine).

16. When Scherlinger turns physiognomist, he writes of usually avoiding
the faces of others, since he "would [not] have wished to draw their
glances [*Blicke*]" (IV.2.735).

17. *Le Livre des mille nuits et une nuit,* trans. Dr. J. C. Mardrus (Paris: Char-
pentier et Fasquelle, 1924), 13:291. In the drug protocol of December 18,
1927, Benjamin writes: "I remembered the *1001 Nights*. . . ." (VI.559).

Kasim's wife, too, as greedy as her spouse and sharing his confusion between the treasure and grain, accuses Ali Baba of measuring his gold as "a grain-seller measures grain!" (286).

18.   *Das Gleiche* can also be translated as "the same."

Five: The Monstrosity of Translation

1.   Translated as "The Task of the Translator," in Walter Benjamin, *Illuminations,* ed. Hannah Arendt, trans. Harry Zohn (New York: Schocken, 1969), 69–82. Harry Zohn's lucid translations have made a decidedly meaningful contribution to the understanding of Benjamin by an English-speaking audience. The criticism that appears here and there in my text should be recognized more as a play between possible versions than as a claim to establish a more "correct" translation.

2.   The translations, such as they are, are my own.

3.   Benjamin's essay could well be read as an ironical commentary on the traditional reading of "Correspondances" in "On Some Motifs in Baudelaire" (1.2.638–48), where Benjamin reinterprets the "correspondances" as a temporal displacement bound to the "essentially distant," the "inapproachability" of the cult image.

For a general discussion of the concept of symbolic language which the Baudelaire piece poses, see Paul de Man, "The Rhetoric of Temporality," in *Blindness and Insight* (Minneapolis: University of Minnesota Press, 1971), as well as Walter Benjamin, *Ursprung des deutschen Trauerspiels* (1.1:336–37, 342).

4.   The connection between original and translation "may be called a natural one," Benjamin writes, "more precisely a connection of life [*ein Zusammenhang des Lebens*]" (IV.1.10). To make his meaning clear, he repeats the syllable *Leben* sixteen times in the course of the paragraph, and midway through clears it of its traditional meaning. The "life" to which translations are bound is itself woven into textual history: "The sphere of life must ultimately be fixed in history, not in nature. . . . Thus, the task arises for the philosopher to understand all natural life through the more encompassing life of history" (IV.1.11).

5.   Harry Zohn translates "Entfaltung" as "flowering"—and understandably so, for this extension of the metaphorical web is a natural one. It is not, however, Benjamin's.

6. "Translation is then ultimately expedient for the expression of the innermost relation of languages to one another. It cannnot possibly reveal [*offenbaren*] this hidden relationship itself, cannot possibly establish it [*herstellen*], but can perform it [*darstellen*] by a germinating or intensive realization" (IV.1.12).

7. This chapter, "The Monstrosity of Translation," was first published in 1975, and my comments on Zohn's translation were (and remain) based on the version he published in the 1969 Schocken ed. of Benjamin, *Illuminations,* ed. Arendt. Zohn's translation as it appears in the 1996 Harvard University edition has, it is worth remarking, been reworked.

8. "Here as in every other essential regard, Hölderlin's translations, especially those of the two Sophoclean tragedies, present themselves as a confirmation. The harmony of the languages is so deep in them, that the meaning [*Sinn*] is touched by the language only as an Aeolian harp is touched by the wind. Hölderlin's translations are originary images [*Urbilder*] of their form: they relate themselves even to the most perfect translations of their texts as the originary-image to the example" (IV.1.20–21). ("Hierfür wie in jeder andern wesentlichen Hinsicht stellen sich Hölderlins Übertragungen, besonders die der beiden Sophokleischen Tragödien, bestätigend dar. In ihnen ist die Harmonie der Sprachen so tief, daß der Sinn nur noch wie eine Äolsharfe vom Winde von der Sprache berührt wird. Hölderlins Übersetzungen sind Urbilder ihrer Form; sie verhalten sich auch zu den vollkommensten Übertragungen ihrer Texte als das Urbild zum Vorbild.")

9. Benjamin, "Task of the Translator," trans. Zohn, 78.

10. Zohn's translation is perhaps more logical, certainly more optimistic, but does not quite form itself in detail according to the strange mode of Benjamin's meaning: "In the same way a translation, instead of resembling the meaning of the original, must lovingly and in detail incorporate the original's mode of signification, thus making both the original and the translation recognizable as fragments of a greater language, just as fragments are part of a vessel" (ibid.).

11. Gershom Scholem, in writing about "On the Concept of History," relates the figure of the angel of history to the *Tikkun* of the Lurianic Kabbalah. "Yet at the same time, Benjamin has in mind the kabbalistic concept of the *Tikkun,* the messianic restoration and mending which patches together and restores the original Being of things, shattered and

corrupted in the 'Breaking of Vessels,' and also [the original Being of] history" ("Walter Benjamin und sein Engel," in *Zur Aktualität Walter Benjamins* [Frankfurt: Suhrkamp, 1972], 132–33).

If Scholem recognizes the failure of the angel of history to carry out this task, he nevertheless sees evidence of this redemption elsewhere in Benjamin (ibid., 133–34).

Scholem might have turned to "The Task of the Translator," where the image of the broken vessel plays a more direct role. Harry Zohn's (mis)translation of this passage (quoted in note 10, above) along with Benjamin's carefully articulated messianic rhetoric seem to speak here of the successful realization of the *Tikkun*. Yet, whereas Zohn suggests that a totality of fragments are brought together, Benjamin insists that the final outcome of translation is still "a broken part." In the Lurianic doctrine, then, translation would never progress beyond the stage of the *Shevirath Ha-Kelim*. (For a description of this "Breaking of Vessels" as Benjamin knew it, see Gershom Scholem, *Major Trends in Jewish Mysticism* [New York: Schocken, 1973].) In the closing passage of "The Task of the Translator," the messianic valorization of the Holy Scriptures ironically serves to usher in the fundamental fragmentation that interlinear translation performs.

12. Benjamin speaks at length of the concept of *Kritik* in the early Romantics in *Der Begriff der Kunstkritik in der deutschen Romantik* (1.1.11–122).

Six: Emergency, Break

1. But also of "Doctrine" and even of "of."

2. The question of the occult enters Benjamin's work from a number of different directions and in different forms. On the one hand, it seems allied with surrealism (II.1.307; s, 189). Elsewhere, it has a more somber role to play. See, for example, "Erleuchtung durch Dunkelmänner" (III.356).

3. Benjamin uses it in this sense in "Towards the Image of Proust," writing that Proust's "most precise, most evident cognitions sit on their objects like insects on leaves, blossoms, and branches, betraying nothing of their existence until a spring, a beat of wings, a jump [or 'sentence' (*Satz*)] show the startled observer that an incalculable individual life had imperceptibly crept into an alien world. . . . The true reader of Proust is constantly jarred by such shocks" (II.1.317–18; IP, 208).

4. Benjamin's father was a merchant (VII.2.531), and Benjamin tried to become a teacher.

5. In a similar remark, Benjamin writes: "The classless society is not the final aim of the progress of history, but rather its so often unsuccessful, finally accomplished interruption [*Unterbrechung*]" (I.3.1231).

6. How can one fail to hear the phrase that was still something of a joke in Benjamin's time: ontogeny recapitulates phylogeny?

7. What is here "meditation" [*Besinnung*] becomes "insight" in "On the Mimetic Faculty."

8. What the reader expects is that the tiny segment of consciously perceived similarities are to the innumerable unconsciously perceived similarities like the small tip of the iceberg to the enormous underwater block.

9. One need only think of "Towards the Image of Proust" or "Myslowitz, Braunschweig, Marseille."

10. If Benjamin offers us the *constellation* in an elaborate simile and does so in the course of an unrepeatable, ungraspable moment, this is hardly the case for the *Gestirnstand* (translated as "star cluster" to distinguish it from *Konstellation*): "The star cluster displays [*darstellt*] a characteristic unity and (it is) *first* in their operation in the star cluster that the characters of the individual planets are recognized" (II.1.206; DS, 66). Fixed object of imitation, set in a temporality of sequence, the star cluster, or *Gestirnstand*, promises a unity and the possibility of knowledge [*Erkenntnis*] quite different from the constellation. The latter is formed by the addition, the coming along of, the apparent perceiver, the astrologer, who therefore can never perceive or cognize [*erkennen*] the constellation as a fixed unity outside himself.

11. The connection between reading, writing, and the constellation is, in fact, the culmination point of the essay. There, reading and writing are imbedded in the rapid temporality, the flash we have seen to take place in the constellation.

12. For the point of the critical gestures of comparison—say, of the iceberg and also of the constellation—is precisely that they do *not* work, disrupting, rather, the order and reason we have always assigned to language in relation to that which it names and the relation of the perceiver to the perceived. Thus, in the simile of the iceberg it is the tension among the terms that drives the comparison displacing any conception of ordered likeness of the particular pairs. The simile of the constella-

tion is such that the astrologer, proposed as an image to explain the perception of similarities in general, stands in no position to perceive the whole as "originary totality" or "unity" (II.1.206; DS, 66).

13. Whereas I only touch upon points of similarity among "Doctrine of the Similar," "Towards the Image of Proust," and "On the Concept of History," the publication of Stephane Moses' "Eingedenken und Jetztzeit—Geschichtliches Bewußtsein im Spätwerk Walter Benjamins" (*Memoria: Vergessen und Erinnern* [Munich: Wilhelm Fink, 1993], 385–405) has anticipated much I have attempted to suggest. He develops the relationship among these essays with far more precision and far more breadth.

14. The essay entitled "Surrealism" is important to include in this constellation. There, the question of revolution is raised, together with language and the image.

15. See also *Das Passagen-Werk* (V.1.595) for a variation of this passage.

16. Thus, in reading the following passage: "If, from different languages, one orders words that mean the same around what is meant as their middle point, it would have to be investigated how they all—while often not possessing the slightest similarity to one another—are similar to that which is meant at their center" (II.1.207; DS, 67), Werner Hamacher writes:

> This middle point is first constituted by the arrangement of the particular words of the language, and it must be thought of as their dynamic result and as itself a linguistic being. The likeness Benjamin speaks of is thus neither the likeness between a sign and a thing, nor that between a sign and a representation, but rather the likeness between the words—and these words are never reduced to their sign character—of virtually all languages, on the one hand, and their configuration, on the other. This likeness does not *persist*, is not static and has no consistency, but is generated—and indeed without pre-given rules—by each new configuration "every time in a completely new, original and non-deducible way" (II.1.208).

Hamacher, "The Word *Wolke*—If It Is One," in *Benjamin's Ground*, ed. Rainer Nägele (Detroit: Wayne State University Press; 1988), 152–53.

17. Benjamin cites Leonhard, and citation as "On the Concept of History" insists, is yet another form that the constellation might assume. Thus, he will speak of the encounter between present and past not only as

constellation but also as citation (1.2.,694; TH, 254). In *Das Passagen-Werk* something similar takes place, in the juxtaposition, for example of [N 10a, 3] (which speaks of the constellation and the dialectical image) and [N 11,3]: "To write history also means to *cite* history. Implicit in the concept of citing, however, is that any particular historical object be ripped out of its context" (V.1.595; N, 67).

18. Thus, one can with philological acuity find names for the sources of Benjamin's "conception and spontaneity." Winfried Menninghaus in his learned *Walter Benjamins Theorie der Sprachmagie* (Frankfurt: Suhrkamp, 1980), 38, speaks of A. W. Schlegel, Friedrich Schlegel, Novalis, and Humboldt, and also of the early Romantics in general. To these one could add the name of Kant.

19. This is perhaps not unlike what in "Doctrine of the Similar" Benjamin will speak of as the force of *Verspannung* ("tension"), which ironizes conventional, abstract concepts of identity and similarity, a force that makes *beth* have the name of a house as well as vice versa.

20. In "Sokrates," however, written in the same year as "On Language as Such" (1916), "immaculate conception" has its place (II.1.131).

21. What follows is a reading, not of Benjamin's thinking "as it really was" (1.2.695; TH, 255), but rather, of what was never written. No doubt it makes more sense to hear in "conception" a citation of Schlegel, Humboldt, and Kant than of the New Testament, as I will suggest. My reading might be called a gesture that has midrashic affinities, or more in Benjamin's terminology, speak of its method as "performance as detour" (1.1.208). This method of reading may not, therefore, reveal the true sources of Benjamin's thoughts so much, perhaps, as perform a new version of them.

22. *The Catholic Encyclopedia* (New York: Robert Appleton, 1910), 7:675. See also *New Catholic Encyclopedia* (New York: McGraw-Hill, 1967), 7:378.

23. An exceptional analysis of the implications of typology for theory of reading is Jill Robbins's *Prodigal Son/Elder Brother* (Chicago: University of Chicago, 1991). There, by way of introduction, she writes, "The Christian tradition already includes an account of the Judaic in its assertion of the *figural* relationship between the two testaments, namely, the idea that the Old Testament anticipates and is fulfilled by the New" (1).

24. *Catholic Encyclopedia*, 7:675. Rainer Nägele, *Theater, Theory, Speculation* (Baltimore: Johns Hopkins University Press, 1991), 83, in an interpreta-

tion of Christian allegorization both less restrained and no doubt shrewder than mine, attributes to it some of the radical force I attribute only to Benjamin's reading.

25. That is, in the two turns of indirection in "Doctrine of the Similar" that lead to understanding the astrological moment both as the defining moment of human birth and as the production of the constellation.

> But [*aber*] if mimetic genius really was a life-determining force of the ancients, then it is hardly possible not to attribute the full possession of this gift . . . to the newborn.
>
> The moment [*Augenblick*] of birth that should be decisive here is, however [*aber*], an instant [*Nu*]. That detours the glance to another peculiarity in the realm of similarity. Its perception is in every case bound to an [instantaneous] flash. (II.1.206; DS, 66)

26. How could it be insignificant in this connection that he names his own gesture, it too a naming: "Perhaps it is daring . . . *to name* verse 2.20 in its second part in this context. " (II.1.149; OLaS, 324, emphasis added).

27. *The Anchor Bible Dictionary* (New York: Doubleday, 1992), 1:62.

28. The even more obvious reading of the passage in its context in "On the Mimetic Faculty" is that Benjamin writes of a historical moment (with what irony should be evident) before writing had appeared on the scene.

29. "Historical materialist" in the thoroughly foreign and elusive sense of that term in "On the Concept of History."

Index

Library of Congress Cataloging-in-Publication Data
Jacobs, Carol.
    In the language of Walter Benjamin / Carol Jacobs.
        p.   cm.
    Includes bibliographical references and index.
    ISBN 0-8018-6031-8 (alk. paper)
    1. Benjamin, Walter, 1892–1940—Criticism and interpretation.
I. Title.
PT2603.E455Z679   1999
838'.91209—dc21   98-42416
                                                                 CIP